DEDICATION

I take this opportunity to dedicate this book to my parents, family members and brothers whose constant support and motivation always guided me in the positive direction.

Next Century- India Century.

INDIA AT A GLANCE

RAJENDRA KUMAR SHARMA

ISBN:	Softcover	978-1-4828-6836-4
	eBook	978-1-4828-6835-7

Print information available on the last page.

To order additional copies of this book, contact
Partridge India
000 800 10062 62
orders.india@partridgepublishing.com

www.partridgepublishing.com/india

CONTENTS

PREFACE

It is a proud feeling for me to publish and present the first edition of my book, "India At A Glance". The book is being published through reputed publisher Partridge India.

The book, which has hit the stands, has been written with an exceptionally optimistic outlook about India. There is no ill-intention to undermine or give any sweeping opinion about Government or Individual. If anything is allowed to happen that is due to circumstances prevailing at a particular time and customary ethical and moral values of countrymen.

The issues raised and discussed in this book have been hunting me since long. I have tried to highlight all issues facing the country so that the enlightened public may rise to the occasion and help resolve them to make India a country free from the evils like Corruption, nepotism, population, poverty, unemployment and communal intolerance, etc. These problems of the 20th century have continued in the current century as well.

The endeavour of this book is to educate the students of all the educational institutions and disciplines, including competitive examinations, and persons who are interested in understanding the social, economic and political problems of India.

Immediately after Independence, the country had to face wars with China and Pakistan and communal disturbances, rehabilitation of millions of people, migration of people, problem of starvation, food shortage. All these problems were born out of the slavery under British rule, and further compounded by a poor economy. The freedom from the British brought with Poverty, Population explosion, social and political disparities coupled with corruption.

A good chunk of the Budget was spent on maintaining communal harmony, and dealing with poverty, corruption and other problems. In spite of difficult time, India tried its best to address these problems and, to some extent, it succeeded.

Now India has entered the 21st century, it is a matter of respite that the "country has got a will power for the eradication of its all evils. I am sure, by the year 2030, India will be able to prevail over all the problems with the help and contribution of the younger generation.

My book highlights the entire predicament and its effect in future.

I am very thankful to my wife Mrs. Yogeshwari Sharma, M.A. (Political Science), and my sons, Karan Sharma, Master of Science in Artificial Intelligence and Computer Science, and Pranav Sharma, B.Tech (IT), who helped me write down the book.

Time-to-time guidance from them encouraged me to complete the entire writing.

I am very thankful to all of my friends especially Ramesh Chaudhary, EX-News Editor, Chandigarh Tribune for editing of book.

I am also thankful to various computer sites, the Central-State Library, Chandigarh, and the staff of the reading room for their wholehearted support to me and my research on the subjects.

Rajendra Kumar Sharma
8.rajan@gmail.com

B.A (Honours) Economics
M.A. (Public Administration)

Fellow of Insurance Institute of India, Bombay

....

Chapter 1

BIRTH OF INDEPENDENT INDIA

On the eve of the First Independence Day, Jawaharlal Nehru, India's first Prime Minister, said, "Long years ago we made a tryst with destiny, and now the time comes when we shall redeem our pledge, not wholly or in full measure, but very substantially. At the stroke of midnight hour, when the world sleeps, India will awake to life and freedom. A moment comes which comes but rarely in history, when we step out from the old to new, when an age ends and when the soul of nation long suppressed. We end today a period of misfortune and India discovers herself again. Freedom and power bring responsibility."

These are the emotional words which were expressed by Jawaharlal Nehru and more exciting WORDS were "The past is over and it is the future that becomes us new". Its secret meanings again explained by Nehru, "And so we have to labour and to work hard, to give reality to our dreams."

Jawaharlal Nehru also declared, "The service of India means the service of millions who suffer. It means the ending of poverty and ignorance and disease and inequality of opportunity. The ambition of the greatest man of our generation has been to wipe every tear from every eye. That may be beyond us, but as long as there are tears and suffering, so long our work will not be over."

While analyzing the speech, it is clear that dreams of India were immense and broad.

Pt. Nehru is the maker of modern democratic and peaceful vision of India. He is the founder of non-alignment movement. Nation building was at the heart of Nehru's activities especially in the field of planning, community development and atomic energy. He is the angel of piece and his piece loving messages are the backbone of his personality which shows his strength of character.

Gandhi Ji, who has a great contribution to free India, cannot be forgotten and will be remembered as a grand saint in coming centuries. Due to inspiration of this great saint of the 19th century, We, the people of India, irrespective of any religion, caste and creed, made every endeavor with our core of heart for liberalizing India by non-violence methods, have written a story in golden words which will be remembered in coming era.

The period of 1920 to 1947 may be term as Gandhian Era in Indian Politics. The grand saint of India was born on 2nd October 1869 at Porbandar in Gujarat. All the well-known movements like Non-cooperation movement (1920), Civil Disobedience Movement (1930) Quite India Movement (1942) are in the name of Gandhiji. It was a quite India Movement which gave a great jolt to Britishers and they were asked to leave India immediately and they had to leave.

Gandhiji will be remembered as great saint, social reformer, truthful and religious person. "Raghupati Raghav Raja Ram Patit Pavan sita Ram" will be in the core of heart of all Indians and other communities. The persons who came in his contact with him were deeply influenced by his personality. A film after 35 years of Independence (1992) by Sir Richard Attenborough on "Gandhi", is eighth highest Oscar winning of all time claiming eight awards from 11 nominations. This shows the popularity of Gandhiji not only in India and United Kingdom but also in the whole world. He worked whole of his life for Non-violence, Hindu-Muslim unity, untouchability, upliftment of poor and harijans.

A gloom day came when Nathu Ram Godsey shot him dead on 30th January 1948. His sacrifice to the nation will be written in Golden words. Such Mahatams came in the world after thousands and thousands of years.

When the time was of our festivity and dancing, we could not know that a series of challenges were approaching and we had to face them at the cost of our economy. The problems that throated us were relief and rehabilitation of millions of displaced persons and to establish peace and security. The question is whether we could face such challenge and achieve our dreams after 1947 or still stand there. The series of challenges are:

PARTITION OF INDIA

Lord Mountbatten announced the partition of India and declared it separate nation from British. On 14th August 1947, Pakistan became independent nation and on the next day India became Independent. The question is why there was a partition of India? The reasons may be thousands but the fact is "India partitioned". The causes of partition may be dividing and rule policy of Britishers, Demand of Muslims, Hindus and self interest of politicians, whatsoever, the causes, the fact cannot be forgotten that it was the saddest moment of history of India. The people who were living together, fighting together, they failed to beat the feeling of harmony and unity among themselves. Thus challenges of new nations started from Communal disharmony.

The first instant challenge faced by our country was Partition of India. The impact of Partition was very painful and sore. The result of Partition was bloodshed and that too in the form of communal brutality. For Gandhi Ji, Partition had been so unacceptable that they had refused to acknowledge the legitimacy of the power of this state. He went on protest, padyatras, undertook a fast unto death and demonstrated his dismay in other ways. To quote from Mushirul Hasan (2002: 213-214), they argued that "the price of freedom was Partition". Nehru and all other leaders thus accepted that the price of Independence was Partition and what was now needed was protection of the borders of new nation-state.He also realized even as the bloody partition that foreshadowed the division of the subcontinent that unlike Pakistan that had opted Muslim land, India would remain a country of many religions and it was continuing endeavour to make the large Muslim majority that remained behind feel at home.

The transfer of power from the British, though smooth and orderly, was accompanied with Partition which gave rise to communal violence and migration to India of millions displaced persons. The aftermath of Partition has displaced about 10 millions to 15 millions of people, besides thousands were killed and injured. Curbing the communal violence was a hard task for the Government. People in their own country were called as "Refugees".

The exact meaning of refugees is that "It is a person who is outside his or her country or origin or habitual residence because they have suffered on account of race, religion, nationality and politically opinion". Thus, the citizens of own country have a label of Refugee which was not only painful but also shameful. I know the plight of my parents and grandparents who came from a small village of Pakistan and till the end of their life they lived with the horrible memories of "Journey to India". Accepting the challenge and with the help of the Government of India, they could establish themselves. Whenever they sat together with us and grandchildren, they would usually tell us about the sufferings of those innocent children and families who were deserted during transit.

en.wikipedia.org/wiki/Religious_violence_in_India #/media/
File:Emergency_trains_crowded_with_desperate_refugees.jpg

Partition and communal violence were great challenges for free India. When India was made free, India declared herself as Secular State, whereas Pakistan declared them as Muslim State. The secular approach of India helped alleviate fears and ease angry feelings. Thus, divide-and-rule policy of the British Government had given long-term effects in both countries' economy. After Partition of India, economy was in a very bad shape and the country had to face food shortage. It was a gigantic task before the Government to make food and shelter available to millions of people in free India.

Mr R.K. Shanmukhan Chetty, the then Finance Minister, presented the Union Budget for a period of 7-1/2 months from 15th August, 1947 to 31st March, 1948. The Budget speech clearly said, "Whatever might be the immediate political justification of Partition, its economic consequences must be fully appreciated if the two dominions are to safeguard the interest of ordinary man in both the new states". Though a number of committees and sub-committees were appointed to deal with the problem arising out of Partition, it was not an easy task to complete their job within the specified period.

As the newly formed Government was inexperienced and resources were not too much as there was a deterioration in the economic situation in the country, it further aggravated with the large-scale disturbances which burst suddenly, more especially in the Punjab and North-West Frontier Province. The immediate effect of this tragic development diverted the Government's attention from normal activities. The economy of the country was fully shattered, especially in the area of East and West Punjab. Though the Government had taken every possible step to tackle the breakdown of economy and suffering of refugees, yet it imposed a heavy burden on the Central Government Budget.

The Budget of the Central Government for the next few years was materially affected by this unexpected development in the country. The total revenue for the year 1947-48 was estimated at Rs. 171.15 crore and a revenue expenditure of Rs. 197.39 crore. Thus, a net deficit was Rs. 26.24 crore. The major portion i.e. Rs. 92.44 crore went in the account of the defence services, the balance representing with civil expenditure.

The following chart will clear the picture of communal brutality due to dislocation of people:

Name of country	Year	Population	Dislocated person	Expenditure incurred to rehabilitate
India	1941	38.99 crore		
India	1947	33.00 crore	12 millions	22 crore
Pakistan	1947	06.00 crore		

Source: en.wikipedia.org/wiki/Partition_of_India & First Budget speech

The above statistics shows that India's population in 1941 was around 39 crores. After partition 33 crores remained in India and another 6 crore became part of Pakistan. There were dislocation of persons around 10/15 millions, which was about 4 to 5% of total population of India. To rehabilitate the migrants in Independent India 10-12% of the budget revenue was kept for their welfare for the current year. Keeping in view of the ratio of population of India, migration and limited resources, the ratio of expenditure was kept quite sufficient in the Union budget for well being and rehabilitation of migrants.

CHALLENGES AFTER PARTITION

When a new baby is born, the first question that comes in our mind is how to look after the baby. If he is critical, then extra care is necessary so that he may survive. The same was the case with free India.

Newly formed Government had to face the first and foremost challenge of sudden outburst of communal violence and migration of Hindus and Muslims. Though the number of displaced persons and movement of persons from one border to another were so high, yet the Government had left no stone unturned to keep the situation under control. In view of this, the Government had to incur heavy expenses to control this brutality on Hindus, Sikhs, Muslims and Bengalis.

To give the reality to Mahatma Gandhi's dream, India started labour and hard work for the development of the country. To achieve this, India set up a Planning Commission in March 1950 by a resolution of the Government of India which defined the scope of its work.

The task of the Planning Commission was:

- To make an assessment of the material, capital and human resources of the country, including technical, personnel, and to investigate the possibilities of augmenting them, wherever deficient,
- To formulate a plan for the most effective and balanced utilization of the country's resources.
- To determine priorities and define the stages in which the plan should be carried out and proposed the allocation of resources for the due completion of each stage.

Thus the main purpose of planning commission was to increase the standard of living of people by using maximum national resources, to increase production and to create employment opportunities for all.

The planning commission is entrusted with the responsibility of making assessment of all resources in the country, augmenting defi cient resources, formulating plans for the most effective balances utilization of resources and determining priorities

The first and foremost challenge was how to rehabilitate the migrated people as the rehabilitation of displaced persons presents numerous special problems. The programme of rehabilitation was an integral part of five year plans and kept under constant review, in particular, for meeting the exigencies of the changing situations in respect of displaced persons from East Pakistan.

REHABILITATION OF DISPLACED PERSONS

According to the 1951 Census, about 7 to 15 million persons had moved into India in search of permanent homes, 4 to 9 millions from West Pakistan and about 2 to 6 millions from East Pakistan.

The displaced persons from West Pakistan are dispersed over the Punjab, PEPSU, Delhi, Uttar Pradesh, Saurashtra, Bombay, Madhya Pradesh, Madhya Bharat, Ajmer, Bhopal and Rajasthan. They are more or less evenly divided between urban and rural avocations.

Although 2 to 6 million Hindus had moved into India from East Pakistan by the beginning of 1951, still seven or eight million Hindus are living there. The influx continues; Though the exact data of migration is not available, in reply to question No. 1256 on 28th July, 2015, Shri Kiran Riji Ju, Minister of State for Home Affairs, stated that since 1947 about 1,00,18,173 displaced persons migrated from Pakistan (both erstwhile West Pakistan and East Pakistan) to India and settled in different States of the country and about 47,000 migrants from erstwhile Pakistan are settled in Jammu & Kashmir after Partition in 1947. State-wise annexure is as under:

Annexure 1 (1947-1958)

S. No.	Name of State	Number of migrants
1	Andhra Pradesh	4,000
2	Bombay	4,15,000
3	Delhi	5,01,000
4	Himachal Pradesh	5,000
5	Madras	9,000

6	Madhya Pradesh	2,13,000
7	Mysore	7,000
8	Punjab	27,37,000
9	Rajasthan	3,73,000
10	Uttar Prdesh	4,86,000
11	Andaman and Nicobar	4,000
12	Assam	4,87,000
13	Bihar	67,000
14	Manipur	2,000
15	Odhisa	12,000
16	West Bengal	31,61,000
17	Tripura	3,74,000
18	Jammu and Kashmir	47,215
	TOTAL	89,04,215

About 11 million migrants settled in India after 1958 in different parts of India.`

URBAN RESETTLEMENT

The problem of urban resettlement has been one of the great complexities, chiefly because of the essential differences in the economic pattern of the incoming and outgoing population. This difference has been more marked in the case of displaced persons from West Pakistan. While the Muslim migrants from the Punjab, PEPSU, Delhi, etc., were often labourers or artisans, with a comparatively low standard of life, the incoming non-Muslims were largely industrialists, businessmen, petty shopkeepers or those belonging to the white-collar professions and used to much better living conditions. Secondly, as the urban economy in India, as in any other under-developed country, does not offer much scope.

EXPENDITURE ON REHABILITATION

The following data will clear the picture on expenditure on Rehabilitation:

(Rupees in crore)

	1951-52	1952-53	1953-54	Total
Rural resettlement	3.88	4.04	2.80	10.72
Urban housing	16.11	14.34	12.00	42.45
Urban loans (other than R.F.A.)	2.42	3.37	3-50	9.29
Loans by rehabilitation finance administration	1.88	2.05	3.00	6.93
Technical training, education and other schemes	4.88	4.01	6.70	15.59
Total	29.17	27.81	28.00	84.98

Up to the 31ist March, 1952 the Government had incurred a total expenditure of Rs. 90.54 crores on the rehabilitation—as distinct from relief—of displaced persons. Rs. 27-81 crores are proposed to be spent during 1952-53 and Rs. 28-00 crores during 1953-54.

To deal with the problem, Rehabilitation and finance administration was also set up to rehabilitate to displaced persons. It was set up by the Government after partition supplements other government activities for the rehabilitation of displaced person. As per Press Information Bureau note dated 3-8-54, till 1953-54, it is estimated that total expenditure incurred by Central Government for rehabilitation of displaced person amounting to Rs. 201.02 crores. Considerable expenses has also been incurred by Punjab, West Bengal and other states where displaced persons have migrated to.

Post-Partition history confirms that it led to a population transfer of more than 11 million people between both the newly created nations and death of about 1 million persons. In addition to this, India experienced the problem of food shortage, articles, transport, severe inflation, relief and rehabilitation of millions of displaced persons, winning over several hundred princely states so as to achieve political consolidation and national unity. The threat that India faced was being split into bits, endangering the national unity.

With the transfer of power, the states were left free to decide their future relationship with India. These princely states were large as well as small. The fate of unity hanged in the balance. Fortunately, India had the Iron Man for this job, named Sardar Vallabhbhai Patel. By clever negotiations conducted by the Sardar, the princely states were persuaded to accede to the Indian Union.

Thus, in the difficult circumstances, the Government had moderately or totally worked out the requirement of accommodation for displaced persons by the end of 1953-54. It was estimated that over 80,000 persons received employment through employment exchanges, the Ministry of Railways and other organizations. Similarly, more emphasis was laid on technical education and vocational training and to grant loans.

In view of the above analysis, it is clear that the Government of India had sincerely dealt the problem of rehabilitation and as per available figures, the total expenditure might be around Rs. 300 crore for the wellbeing of migrants, which was sufficient in view of the limited resources available with the Government at that time. We have no hesitation to record that our all leaders like Jawaharlal Nehru, Sardar Patel, Opposition leaders and all other distinguished leaders, public of India, religious and other

CHAPTER 2

START-UP PROCESS OF INDEPENDENT INDIA

The start-up formation of free India was in progress before 1947. The first and foremost priority of India was to have its own Constitution.

The Constitution of a country lays down the basic structure of the political system under which its people are to be governed. In other words, the Constitution is a guiding principle of Government and dictionary of all bylaw-related solutions.

It was M.N. Roy, a pioneer of the Communist Movement in India and an Advocate of democracy who put forward the idea of framing Constitute Assembly for the first time in 1934. In the year 1935, Indian National Congress officially demanded for formation of Constituent Assembly. After the outbreak of the war in 1939, the demand for a constituent assembly was reiterated and on 19th Nov. 1939, Gandhi wrote an article "The Only Way" in which he expressed the view that Constitute Assembly alone can produce a constitution indigenous to the country and truly and fully representing the will of the people" The demand for Constitutes Assembly was accepted in 1940. In light of this demand, Crisp Mission came to India in 1942 under the leadership of Sir Stafford Cripps with proposal for future

Government of India . Two major Parties Congress and Muslim League could come to anagreement. Some of the proposals were, to establish a constitution making body, an interim Government after the cessation of war, thirdly dominion status, fourthly an Indian federation consisting of all provinces and Princely Indian states but freedom was given to Provinces and States to return their constitution.

Cripps proposals were rejected by Congress, Muslims and other section in India on various grounds. After rejecting such proposals, Mahatma Gandhi launched quite India movement in 1942. Simla conference was held in the year 1945 at the instance of viceroy, Lord Wavell, which was also rejected by Congress. Thus talks were failed.

A popular Government consisting of five representative of the Congress, five of Muslim League and one each from other communities came into existence.

The constituent Assembly was constituted in November 1946 with 389 members, 296 representing the provinces and 93 from princely states. The first historical session of Indian Constitute Assembly took place on December 9, 1946 and elected Dr Sachhidanand Sinha, the oldest member of Assembly as the provisional president. Dr. Rajendra Prasad was elected as President of Constituent Assembly on December 11, 1946

Though the strength of the Assembly was 296 members, the first historical session was attended by 210 members following the withdrawal of Muslim League members.

Nehru moved the famous objectives resolution on 13th December and it was discussed for a week and they postponed the adoption of the objectives resolution as the members of the Muslim League were absent and the princely states were to join the Assembly. The third session of the Assembly took place from 28 April to 2 May 1947.

Then came Mountbatten Plan of 1947. On 20th Feb 1947, the British Government announced its intention to transfer power of British India to the people of India by June 1948 and also issued a statement on 3rd June 1947 declaring the intention of partition of India. There was no other alternative for the Congress except to accept the proposal for partition of India. The Muslim league and other communities also accepted the same.

The Constituents Assembly of India came into being in 1947 and it held its first meeting on 9th day of December 1946 and on August 14, 1947, it assembled as Sovereign Constituent Assembly of dominion of India. After it had been in session for some days, a beautiful worded draft of the objective resolution casted and everything i.e. sovereignty, justice, social, political, economic and equality, freedom of thought, expression, belief, faith worship was guaranteed to the people along with adequate *s*afeguard to minorities, backward and tribal areas. Thus, this resolution gave to the assembly guiding principles

The need of the Constitute Assembly to have a constitution which is flexible and vibrant in keeping with the changing circumstances.

For framing the Constitution, the Constituent Assembly appointed a number of committees like Union Constitution Committee, Union Power Committee, Committees on Fundamental Rights and Minorities, etc. to look into various aspects. These committees were headed by Nehru and Patel. The committees worked hard and produced valuable reports. The first draft was prepared in

1947 by the Advisory Branch of the Office of the Constituent Assembly under Sir B.N. Rau.

The Constituent Assembly On 29th August, 1947, appointed Dr B.R. Ambedkar as Chairman of Drafting Committee of the Constitution.

MAKING OF CONSTITUTION

A Draft Committee for the Constitution of India was formed under the Chairmanship of Dr B.R. Ambedkar. The members of the committee were:

- Dr. B.R. Ambedkar, Chairman
- Sh. K.M. Munshi (ex-Home Minister, Bombay)
- Sh. Alladi Krishnaswami Iyer (ex-Advocate-General)
- N. Gopalaswami Ayenger (Member of the Nehru Cabinet)
- Sh. B.L. Mitter (ex-Advocate-General of India)
- Mr. Saadullah (ex-Chief Minister of Assam, Muslim League Member)
- Sh. D.P. Khaitan (Lawyer)

The Constitutional Adviser was Sir Bengal Narsing Rau.

The Draft Constitution of India prepared by the Draft Committee was submitted to the President of the Constituent Assembly on 21st February, 1948. After considering various comments, criticism and suggestions, the Draft Constitution was submitted to the President of the Constituent Assembly on 26th October, 1948.

The second reading of the Constitution was completed on 16th November, 1949, and on the next day the Constituent Assembly took up the third reading with a motion by Dr. Ambedkar "that the Constitution as settled by the Assembly be passed."

The motion was adopted on 26th November, 1949, and thus on that day, the people of India, in the Constituent Assembly adopted, enacted and gave to themselves the Constitution of the Sovereign Democratic Republic of India. The Constitution was finally signed by members of the Constituent Assembly on 24th January, 1950.

B.R. AMBEDKAR

Dr B.R. Ambedkar was born inMhow (M.P). His father Shri Ramji Maloji Sakpal was Subedar in the Indian Army. He was the youngest and 14th child of his parents. During school days of Ambedkar, there was untouchability all over the country. In 1907, he passed his matriculation examination and in the following year he entered into college, which was affiliated to the Bombay University. After obtaining his degrees in Economics and Political Science from Bombay University, he went to the United State of America.

In October 1916 he enrolled at the London School of Economics where he started working on a doctoral thesis. At the London School of Economics, he took a master's degree in 1921 and in 1923 he took his D.Sc. in economics. Now India is considering to purchase the home in London where Mr. Ambedkar was residing in 1921-22. This house spreads over an area of 2050 sq ft. in prime location of London. Dr. Ambedkar launched active movement against Untouchability.

In nutshell, Dr. Ambedkar was a man of tremendous knowledge, social and political reformer and having a good command over English and thinker.

The other Members of the Draft Committee have also played a vital role in writing the Constitution which is one of the lengthy Constitutions in the world.

The Indian Constitution can be described as a charter of freedom. In keeping with the spirit of pledge, the Constitution is the supremacy of the will of people and their resolve to secure for all citizens justice, social, economic and polity; liberty of thought expression, belief, faith and worship, equality of status and opportunity and to promote among them all fraternity assuring the dignity of the individual and the unity of nation. The words used in the Preamble of our Constitution are some of the noblest having high human values:

WE, THE PEOPLE OF INDIA, are having solemnly resolved to constitute India into a SOVEREIGN SOCIALIST SECULAR DEMOCRATIC REPUBLIC and to secure to all its citizens:

JUSTICE, social, economic and political;

LIBERTY of thought, expression, belief, faith and worship;

EQUALITY of status and of opportunity; and to promote among them all FRATERNITY assuring the dignity of the individual and the unity and integrity of the Nation;

If we go through the above Preamble, we will come across that the words selected for preface were really amazing and flexible, applicable in all states of affair. Thus, the script of the Constitution can reasonably and easily bend. While we analyze the Preamble, the significance of each word will be as under:

WE, THE PEPLE OF INDIA: This testimonial shows that our Constitution makers have given much importance to democracy and independence. We are the supreme, which means sovereign and independent. We, the people, mean India is an independent country. It will not tolerate any internal and external interference of any country or any individual in its matters. The example is of Jammu and Kashmir. India never allowed anybody to interfere in our Kashmir issues. In the Keshvananda Bharti case, Justice Mathew said that the Republic of India was sovereign because it could make or unmake any decision with respect to itself without any interference from outside. (AIR 1973 SC 1461)

SOCIALIST, SECULAR AND DEMOCRATIC

The term socialist means socialism i.e. achievement of socialistic and economic goals through democratic means. It has also been tried to define (45th Amendment) Bill - free from all exploitation.

Our Constitution has given respect to all religions. India is a country of diverse religions and may be termed as land of Gods and spiritualism. Secularism is the backbone of our Constitution. Explaining the meaning of secularism as adopted by India, Alexander Owics has stated, "Secularism is part of the basic of the Indian Constitution and it means equal freedom and respect for all religions. This portion indicates the spirit of our secular democracy. Our Constitution guarantees equality in the matter of religion to all individuals and groups.

India is the only democracy where there is no discrimination in the name of caste, creed and religion."

Abraham Lincoln said, "Democracy is the Government by the people, of the people and for the people." Demo is a Greek word, which means people, and kratos means government or rule. India adopted the people's government. This government is elected by the people and they are responsible to people. The example of democracy is that it successfully conducted sixteen General Elections from 1951 to 2014. In 1951 there were 1,874 candidates. The number rose to 8,251 in the year 2014. Aa many as 814.50 million people were eligible to cast vote. There were 9,30,000 polling booths in India with adequate security.

Although the framework of the Constitution was derived from the Government of India Act, 1935, many provisions were imported from other Constitutions of the world. Some of them are from the Constitutions of Great Britain, the USA, Canada, Ireland, Germany, Australia, South Africa, France and the USSR. Thus, the Indian Constitution can be termed as "Healthy Constitution which is flexible in nature". It is the world's longest Constitution. At the time of commencement, the Constitution had 395 Articles in 22 Parts and 12 Schedules.

During this period, it held 11 sessions, covering a total of 165 days. It consists of almost 80,000 words and took 2 years 11 months and 18 days to debate and enact the constitution. By now the constitution has experienced almost 100 amendments.

The essential features of the Constitution of India are:

- It gives the right to people to exercise universal adult franchise at the age of 21 (Now amended to 18).
- There are open contests to all the constituencies and all the political parties have the right to express freely.

- An independent judiciary, with the Supreme Court as the head and High Courts in the states maintain the rule of law in the country. Any citizen can have the right to go even against the Government.
- Equality before law and the protection of our basic rights are ensured under the Fundamental Rights in the Constitution.
- A unique aspect of the Constitution is Directive Principle of State Policy, which ensures to secure a social order for promotion of the welfare of the people.
- Our Constitution also proclaims that there shall be no discrimination of any sort on the basis of race, colour, caste or creed. Everybody is free to enjoy freedom of religion.
- The nature of the Constitution is rigid as well as flexible. Amendments can be made as per the nature of subject either by a simple majority or a special majority.
- India is a republic and the head is the President.
- It is a combination of Parliament Sovereignty vs. Judicial Supremacy. Both are supreme in their respective spheres.
- From the US constitution, we borrowed principles of judicial review, independence of judiciary, impeachment of President, Vice-President, removal of Supreme Court and High Court Judges.For law making procedure, we looked up to the British Constitution. Similarly, some tips taken from Australian, Canadian and USSR Constitution. Dr B.R. Ambedkar conceded that our constitution is borrowed from the known constitutions.

IMPORTANT FEATURES OF CONSTITUTION

Part	Articles	Chapter/ subject	Brief description of Articles
I	1-4	The Union and its territories	1: Name and territory of the Union. (It also states that Bharat shall be the Union of States). 2: Admission or establishment of new States. 3: Formation of new States and alteration of areas, boundaries or names of the existing States. 4: Laws made under Articles 2 and 3 to provide for the amendment of the First and Fourth Schedules and supplemental, incidental and consequential matters.
II	5-11	Citizenship	5: Citizenship at the commencement of the Constitution. 6: Rights of citizenship of certain persons who have migrated to India from Pakistan. 7: Rights of citizenship of certain migrants to Pakistan. 8: Rights of citizenship of certain persons of Indian origin residing outside India. 9: Persons voluntarily acquiring citizenship of a foreign state not to be citizens. 10: Continuance of the rights of citizenship. 11: Parliament to regulate the right of citizenship by law.

III	12-35	Fundamental Rights	12: Definition 13: Laws inconsistent with or in derogation of the Fundamental Rights. Right to Equality 14: Equality before law. 15: Prohibition of discrimination on grounds of religion, race, caste, sex or place of birth. 16: Equality of opportunity in matters of public employment. 17: Abolition of untouchability. 18: Abolition of titles. Right to Freedom 19: Protection of certain rights regarding freedom of speech, etc. 20: Protection in respect of conviction for offences. 21: Protection of life and personal liberty. 22: Protection against arrest and detention in certain cases. Right Against Exploitation 23: Prohibition of traffic in human beings and forced labour. 24: Prohibition of employment of children in factories, etc. Right to Freedom of Religion 25: Freedom of conscience and free profession, practice and propagation of religion. 26: Freedom to manage religious affairs. 27: Freedom as to payment of taxes for promotion of any particular religion.

			28: Freedom as to attendance at religious instructions or religious worship in certain educational institutions. Cultural and Educational Rights 29: Protection of interests of minorities. 30: Right of minorities to establish and administer educational institutions. 31: Repealed. Saving of certain laws 31A: Saving of laws providing for acquisition of estates, etc. 31B: Validation of certain Acts and regulations. 31C: Saving of laws giving effect to certain directive principles. 31D: Repealed. Right to constitutional remedies 32: Remedies for enforcement of rights conferred by this Part. 32A: Repealed. 33: Power of Parliament to modify the rights conferred by this Part in their application to forces, etc. 34: Restrictions on rights conferred by this Part while martial law is in force in any area. 35: Legislation to give effect to the provisions of this Part.
IV	36-51		Directive Principles of State policy
IV-A	51-A		Fundamental duties

V	52-78	One (Union Executive)	The President and the Vice-President 52: The President of India 53: Executive power of the Union. 54: Election of President. 55: Manner of election of President. 56: Term of office of President. 57: Eligibility for re-election. 58: Qualification for election as President. 59: Conditions of President's office. 60: Oath or affirmation by the President. 61: Procedure for impeachment of the President. 62: Time of holding election to fill vacancy in the office of President and the term of office of person elected to fill casual vacancy. 63: The vice President of India 64: The Vice-President to be ex-officio Chairman of the Council of States. 65: The Vice-President to act as President or to discharge his functions during casual vacancies in the office or during the absence of President. 66: Election of Vice-President. 67: Term of office of Vice-President. 68: Time of holding election to fill the vacancy in the office of Vice-President and the term of office of person elected to fill the casual vacancy. 69: Oath or affirmation by the Vice-President. 70: Discharge of President's functions in other contingencies.

			71: Matters relating to or connected with the election of President or Vice-President. 72: Powers of President to grant pardons, etc., and to suspend, remit or commute sentences in certain cases. 73: Extent of executive power of the Union. Council of Ministers 74: Council of Ministers to aid and advise President. 75: Other provisions as to Ministers. The Attorney-General for India 76: Attorney-General for India. Conduct of government business 77: Conduct of business of the Government of India. 78: Duties of Prime Minister in respect of furnishing of information to the President, etc.
V	79-122	Two (Union Legislature)	79: Constitution of Parliament. 80: Composition of the Council of States. 81: Composition of the House of the People. 82: Readjustment after each census. 83: Duration of Houses of Parliament. 84: Qualification for membership of Parliament. 85: Sessions of Parliament, prorogation and dissolution. 86: Rights of President to address and send messages to Houses. 87: Special address by the President.

			88: Rights of Ministers and Attorney-General in respect of Houses. 89: The Chairman and Deputy Chairman of the Council of States. 90: Vacation and resignation of and removal from the office of Deputy Chairman. 91: Power of the Deputy Chairman or other person to perform the duties of the office of or to act as Chairman. 92: The Chairman or the Deputy Chairman not to preside, while a resolution for his removal from office is under consideration. 93: The Speaker and Deputy Speaker of the House of People. 94: Vacation and resignation of and removal from the offices of Speaker and Deputy Speaker. 95: Power of the Deputy Speaker or another person to perform the duties of the office of or to act as Speaker. 96: The Speaker or the Deputy Speaker not to preside while a resolution for his removal from office is under consideration. 97: Salaries and allowances of the Chairman and Deputy Chairman and the Speaker and Deputy Speaker. 98: Secretariat of Parliament. Conduct of Business 99: Oath or affirmation by members. 100: Voting in Houses, power of Houses to act, notwithstanding vacancies and quorum.

			Disqualification of Members 101: Vacation of seats. 102: Disqualification for membership. 103: Decision on questions as to disqualification of members. 104: Penalty for sitting and voting before making oath or affirmation under Article 99 or when not qualified or when disqualified. Powers, Privileges and Immunities of Parliament and its Members 105: Powers, privileges, etc., of the Houses of Parliament and of the members and committees thereof. 106: Salaries and allowances of members. Legislative Procedure 107: Provisions as to introduction and passing of Bills. 108: Joint sitting of both Houses in certain cases. 109: Special procedure in respect of Money Bills. 110: Definition of Money Bills. 111: Assent to Bills. Procedure in financial matters 112: Annual financial statement. 113: Procedure in Parliament in respect of estimates. 114: Appropriation Bills. 115: Supplementary, additional or excess grants. 116: Votes on account, votes of credit and exceptional grants. 117: Special provisions as to financial Bills.

			Procedure Generally 118: Rules of procedure. 119: Regulation by law of procedure in Parliament in relation to financial business. 120: Language to be used in Parliament. 121: Restrictions on discussion in Parliament. 122: Courts not to inquire into the proceedings of Parliament.
	123	Three	Legislative Powers of President
v	124-147	Four (Union Judiciary)	124: Establishment and constitution of Supreme Court. 125: Salaries, etc., of Judges. 126: Appointment of Acting Chief Justice. 127: Appointment of ad hoc Judges. 128: Attendance of retired Judges at sittings of the Supreme Court. 129: Supreme Court to be a court of record. 130: Seat of Supreme Court. 131: Original jurisdiction of the Supreme Court. 131A: Repealed. 132: Appellate jurisdiction of Supreme Court in appeals from High Courts in certain cases. 133: Appellate jurisdiction of Supreme Court in appeals from High Courts in regard to civil matters. 134: Appellate jurisdiction of Supreme Court in regard to criminal matters. 134A: Certificate for appeal to the Supreme Court.

			135: Jurisdiction and powers of the Federal Court under the existing law to be exercisable by the Supreme Court. 136: Special leave to appeal by the Supreme Court. 137: Review of judgments or orders by the Supreme Court. 138: Enlargement of the jurisdiction of the Supreme Court. 139: Conferment on the Supreme Court of powers to issue certain writs. 139A: Transfer of certain cases. 140: Ancillary powers of Supreme Court. 141: Law declared by Supreme Court to be binding on all courts. 142: Enforcement of decrees and orders of Supreme Court and orders as to discovery, etc. 143: Powers of President to consult Supreme Court. 144: Civil and judicial authorities to act in aid of the Supreme Court. 144A: Repealed. 145: Rules of court, etc. 146: Officers and servants and the expenses of the Supreme Court. 147: Interpretation.
	148-151	Five	Comptroller and Auditor-General of India - Independent Audit Agency
VI	152-237	States and Union Territories	Formation of States, Executive, State Legislatures, Legislative Procedures, High Courts and Subordinate Courts, Procedures in Financial Matters.

VIII	239-241		Union Territories
IX& IXA	243		The Panchayats and Municipalities
X	244		Scheduled and Tribal Area
XI	245-263		Relationship between Union and States
XII	264-300		Finance, property, contracts and suits
	300a		Right to Property
XIII	301-307		Trade and commerce within India
XIV	308-323		Services under the Union and the States
XV	324-329		Adoption of elections under Universal Adult Franchise
XVI	330-342	Special Provision for Certain Classes	330: Reservation of seats for Scheduled Castes and Scheduled Tribes in the House of People. 331: Representation of the Anglo-Indian community in the House of People. 332: Reservation of seats for Scheduled Castes and Scheduled Tribes in the Legislative Assemblies of the States. 333: Representation of the Anglo-Indian community in the Legislative Assemblies of the States. 334: Reservation of seats and special representation to cease after sixty years. 335: Claims of Scheduled Castes and Scheduled Tribes to services and posts. 336: Special provision for Anglo-Indian community in certain services.

			337: Special provision with respect to educational grants for the benefit of the Anglo-Indian community. 338: National Commission for Scheduled Castes. 338A: National Commission for Scheduled Tribes. 339: Control of the Union over the administration of Scheduled Areas and the welfare of Scheduled Tribes. 340: Appointment of a Commission to investigate the conditions of Backward Classes. 341: Scheduled Castes. 342: Scheduled Tribes.
XVII	343-351		Official languages
XVIII	352-360	Emergency Provision	352: Proclamation of Emergency. 353: Effect of Proclamation of Emergency. 354: Application of provisions relating to distribution of revenues while Proclamation of Emergency is in operation. 355: Duty of the Union to protect States against external aggression and internal disturbance. 356: Provisions in case of failure of constitutional machinery in States. 357: Exercise of legislative powers under proclamation issued under Article 356. 358: Suspension of provisions of Article 19 during Emergency.

			359: Suspension of the enforcement of the rights conferred by Part III during Emergency. 359A: Repealed. 360: Provisions as to financial Emergency.
XIX	361-365		Miscellaneous
XX	368		Amendment to Constitution
XXI	369-392		Temporary, transitional and special provision – Special Status of States
XXII	393-395		Short title, commencement, authoritative text in Hindi and repeals.

At present, the Constitution of India consists of 442 Articles, 22 Parts and 12 Schedules.

The First Amendment enacted on 18th JUNE 1951, made several changes to the fundamental rights provisions of the constitution. It provided reasonable restrictions on freedom of speech and expression for maintenance of social order, as no freedom can be absolute or completely. It also provide constitution validity of Zamindari abolition laws.

The Seventh amendment enactedon 1st Nov 1956 relates to reorganization of states on linguistic lines. Abolition of class A,B,C and D states and introduction of Union Territories.

On 5th October 1963, fifteen amendment enacted in constitution. It raised the retirement age of High Court Judges from 60 to 62 years and other minor amendments regarding interpretation of rules.

Until 1971 Privy Purse was a payment made to the royal families of erstwhile princely states as part of their agreements to first integrate with India in 1947, and later to merge their states in 1949 whereby they lost all ruling rights.Th e 26th amendment enacted on 28th December 1971, relates to abolution of privy purse.

As per 31st Amendments, Parliament size was increased from 525 to 545.

Sikkim was formed as a state within Indian Union by 36th Amendment.

The 42nd amendment officially known as (42nd amendment act,1976). Most provisions of the amendment came into effect on 3 January 1977, others were enforced from 1 February 1977.The 42nd Amendment is regarded as the most controversial constitutional amendment in Indian history. It attempted to curtailment of Fundamental Rights, imposes fundamental duties and change to basic structure of the constitution by making India a socialist sector republic. Sometime it is called as Mini constitution. Almost all parts of the Constitution, including the Premable, were changed by the 42nd Amendment, and some new articles and sections were inserted.

The 61st Amendment enacted on 28th March 1989 vide which voting rights have been reduced from 21 to 18 years.

National Commission for SC/ST formed under sixty five amendment act On 12 th March 1990.

The 86th Amendment enacted on 12th December 2002 which provide right of education until the age of 14 and care until the age of six.

99th and 100th amendments relates to formation of National Judicial Commission and exchange of territories with Bangladesh (In process).

FUTURE OF CONSTITUTION

The Indian Constitution and democracy have already entered the 21st century. It is a matter of pride that the Expert Committee has given a democratic Constitution with Fundamental Rights which include Freedom of Speech, Freedom of Expression and Right to Education, etc. The real power of the Constitution lies with ordinary to V.I.P. and newspaper to electronic media people. Though judiciary is playing a vital role to interpret the wording of the Constitution, it is so heavy burdened that it takes a long time to make a decision in the cases. There is a multi-party system in India. During elections, the language used by politicians is not worth to write here. You go anywhere and you will find the law and order problem everywhere. The question is "Why this indiscipline is in India". Is it due to more rights given by the Constitution? Perhaps the answer is negative.

It is understood that Constitution allowed absolute democracy but with discipline. India is proclaimed as a secular state. Our constitution gives freedom of religion to all as per Article 25-28. Articles 25 give freedom of religion to all persons. Articles 26 give freedom to manage religious affairs and institutions. Articles 28 maintains the secular character of Union of India by laying down that in educational institutions run wholly by state funds no religious instructions will be given. Thus Freedom of religion is guaranteed to all, citizens and individuals as well as religious groups. All religions are allowed to flourish. Now the question arises as to why there is religious intolerance, and how the Indian

Society can be made to tolerant. The people may argue that this is due to widespread freedom of everything. If we find out the soul of the constitution, we shall come to know that it granted freedom of everything but with good amount of discipline in every field. No where has it mentioned that indiscipline or trouble can be created by Public or Politicians etc.

On the other hand Part XVIII of the constitution gives powers of proclamation of Emergency by President. He has a power of declaring National, State and Financial Emergency. Thus it is flexible. But if needed, it can do anything.

The vastness of the country and a large population with diversity compelled the makers to provide protection to different communities i.e. minorities, Scheduled Caste and Tribes etc. Thus it can be described as Soverign will be people.

Sh Subhash Kashyap, Constitutional expert said, Constitution in certain area has shown tremendous success and at certain places significant failure". He remarks, the survival of constitution is its greatest success. We are sure that future of constitution lie with its feature of flexibility.

CONCLUSION

It will not be fair to forget the concluding speech of Dr. Rajendra Prasad wherein he stated, "If the people who are elected are capable and men of character and integrity, they would be able to make the best even of a defective Constitution. If they are lacking in these, the Constitution cannot help the country. After all the Constitution, like a machine, is a lifeless thing. India today needs nothing more than a set of honest men who will have the interest of the country before them. We have communal differences, caste differences, language differences and so forth. It requires men of strong character, men of vision, men who will not sacrifice the interests of the country at large for the sake of smaller groups and areas and who will rise over the prejudices which are born of these differences. We can only hope that the country will throw up such men in abundance."

After reading the above paragraph, one thing comes in my mind – "KAHAN GAYE WOH LOG".

These are the concluding remarks which are applicable in today's time. Thus, if we want to maintain democracy for further 1000 years, we have to learn to live in discipline within the limits of constitutional boundaries, otherwise it needs precise amendments.

CHAPTER 3

ON DEVELOPMENT PATH

World War II was over and the British Government principally decided to quit India. They released most of the political prisoners and freedom fighters. Subsequent to freedom, India was faced with initial troubles like Partition, rehabilitation of displaced persons, communal disturbances, Indo-Pakistan War, integration of the country, The Constituent Assembly was engaged in drawing up the Constitution, Jawaharlal Nehru took charge as the first Prime Minister of India in his Cabinet.

PLANNING MODEL

Subsequent to the formation of Cabinet, India was ready for all-around development and to tackle the future problems. To win over these problems, a formal model of planning was adopted and accordingly the Planning Commission was established on 15th March, 1950. The Prime Minister as the ex-officio Chairman, the Commission has a nominated Deputy Chairman, who holds the rank of Cabinet Minister.

The objective of the newly formed Interim Government was to promote employment prospects, raise the standard of living of the people, to increase agricultural production, to eradicate illiteracy from the country by using the resources of the country and also to inculcate confidence among the people. The task of the Planning Commission, among other things, is:

- To make an assessment of the material, capital and human resources of the country, including technical personnel, and investigate the possibilities of augmenting such resources as are found to be deficient;
- To formulate a Plan for the most effective and balanced utilization of the country's resources;
- To determination of priorities, define the stages in which the Plan should be carried out and propose the allocation of resources for the due completion of each stage;
- Indicate the factors which are tending to retard economic development and determine the conditions which, in view of the current social and political situation, should be established for the successful execution of the Plan;
- To determine the nature of the machinery which will be necessary for securing the successful implementation of each stage of the Plan in all its aspects;
- To appraise, from time to time, the progress achieved in the execution of each stage of the Plan and recommend the adjustments of policy and measures that such appraisal may show to be necessary; and
- To make such interim or ancillary recommendations as appear to it to be appropriate either for facilitating the discharge of the duties assigned to it; or on a consideration of the prevailing economic conditions, current policies, measures and development programmes; or on an examination of such specific problems as may be referred to it for advice by the Central or State Governments.

The planning period was started during Nehru regime. The First Five-Year Plan was started in 1951-1956 and Eleventh Plan completed its terms in March 2012 and the Twelfth Plan 2012-2017 is currently in progress. Bharat has chosen the right path to develop India under Five-Year Plans and this experiment was successful to some extent.

Thus Planning Commission was on its job.

FIRST GENERAL ELECTION

The first target of the Government was to conduct General Election. Moreover, it was the duty of the Interim Government to conduct the General Election successfully in the country. To attain this objective, the Election Commission was set up under Article 324 of the Constitution. Article 324 of the Constitution of India has vested in the Election Commission of India the superintendence, direction and control of the entire process for the conduct of elections to Parliament and Legislature of every State and to the offices of President and Vice-President of India. The Election Commission of India is a permanent constitutional body.

The Election Commission was set up in accordance with the Constitution on 25th January, 1950. The Chief Election Commissioner, Shri Sukumar Sen, was appointed to hold the General Election exercise.

The first General Election in India during 1951-52 on the basis of adult franchise involved a good deal of interest and attention in the country as well as abroad. The voting age was fixed as 21 years (now 18 years). The holding of such a vast election was an uphill task and was the example for democracy of a newly created nation. The world eye was on the historical democratic event.

Winston Churchill once said, India would go to wrack and ruin after attaining independence. His prediction proved wrong especially in India's general election. One of the main features of Indian democracy is that transfer of power is always smooth. Till now India has conducted 16 General Elections in a successful manner.

The year-wise election details of the country are as below:

No.of Lok Sabha	Year	Seats	Winning Party *Congress*	Others -winning parties *Others*	Prime Minister India	No. of voters (in millions)
Ist	1951-56	489	364	NA	JawaharLal Nehru	173
2nd	1957-62	494	371	NA	JawaharLal Nehru	193
3rd	1962-67	494	361	NA	JawaharLal Nehru, Gulazari Lal Nanda, Lal Bahadur Shastri Indira Gandhi	216
4th	1967-70	520	283	NA	Indira Gandhi	250
5th	1971-77	518	352	NA	Indira Gandhi	273
6th	1977-79	543	NA	295 (Janata Party)	Morarji Desai Charan Singh	321
7th	1980-84	529	362	NA	Indira Gandhi	356
8th	1985-89	533	414	NA	Rajiv Gandhi	380
9th	1989-91	529	228	229–Janata Dal, BJP, Left parties	V.P. Singh Chandra Shekher	499
10th	1991-96	535	245	NA	PV Narashima Rao	499
11th	1996-98	543	348	United Front	H.D. Devegowda. I.K. Gujral	592
12th	1998-99	544	NA	182- BJP Alliance	Atal Behari Vajpayee	606

13	1999-2004	543	298	NDA	Atal Behari Vajpayee	620
14	2004-09	543	218-UPA		Manmohan Singh	671
15	2009-14	543	261-UPA		Manmohan Singh	716
16	2014-19	543		282-BJP	Narendra Modi	834

At a glance on the above, we shall find that India is a democratic stable country and have a proud of conducting the World biggest electoral exercise as and when need arises.

Until now 16 General Election have been conductedy by various Election Commissions in a doing well approach. Congress and its alliance parties have ruled the country in the first phase from 1947 to 1977. This era may be termed as era of Congress, whereas the Bharatiya Janata Party (BJP), the main Opposition party of India, has ruled the country from 1998 to 2004 under the leadership of Shri Atal Behari Vajpayee and now again in 2014, the BJP had got a thumping majority.

The first Prime Minister of India, Jawaharlal Nehru ruled the country until his death in 27th May 1964 and was succeeded by Lal Bahadur Shastri, who died in the office on 11th January 1966. After the death of Shri Shastri ji, Guljari lal nanda elected as care-taker prime-minister for some days.

Later, Indira Gandhi became the Prime Minister and ruled till 1977. The Congress Government pays heavily for imposition the Emergency in 1975. In the 1977 General Election, the Janta Government came in Power and Morarji Desai headed the Government. After the fall of Morarji Desai Government, Charan Singh formed an interim Government in 1979. In January 1980, Indira Gandhi returned to Power. She was assassinated by the terrorist on 31st October 1984. Rajiv Gandhi succeeded her as Prime Minister.

In 1989 V.P Singh became the Prime Minister of India followed by Chander Sheikher.

On 27th May, 1991, during an election campaign in Tamil Nadu, Rajiv Gandhi was assassinated by LTTE activists but the Congress again formed the Government under the Prime Ministership of PV Narasimha Rao. This was the time when series of Economic Reforms were started which led India on the parth of liberalization and globalization, thus opening various opportunities for the Indian economy.

In 1996 General Election, United front came in power and BJP formed the government as Sh Atal Behari Vajpayee, Prime Minister but the govt. fell down after 13 days.

A 14 parties coaliation, led by the Janata Party with HD Deve Gowda as the Prime Minister governed the country for less than year. When this Government crumbled, Inder Kumar Gujral became the consensus choice for the office of the Prime Minister of United Front. In 1997, the Congress Party withdrew the support from the United Front. In 1998 the BJP emerged as the single largest party with 182 seats and Atal Behari Vajpayee was chosen as Prime Minister.

Due to non cooperation of other parties, Elections were again held in September 1999 and Sh Atal Behari Vajpayee again choses as Prime Minister of India till 2004. Thereafter, Manmohan Singh became the 14th Prime Minister of India on 22nd May 2004 and ruled till 2014.

In 2014 General Election BJP won with thumping majority and got 282 seats. This Government is being led by Shri Narinder Modi, Prime Minister of India.

Thus we can say Indian Political system is the soul of our constitution. No body is above the constitution. Stable Government, fare and free election, pro-poor policies, active judicial participation are the hallmark of our political system. Political factors are loaded in favour of India but they may be utilized fully only when the illiteracy of the masses is eradicated.

Thus, we can say, out of 64 years till 2015, the Congress/UPA ruled the country for 47 years approximately and the remaining period was with other parties. During this period what India has gained and what has lost, needs to be scrutinized.

ERA OF 1951-2015

One thing is rather clear from the above data that we, the people of India, poor or rich, literate or illiterate, young or old and male or female have given the whole credit and shown their confidence in the Congress for their hard work for India's Independence. Election records and the above data speak it.

The most of the period the Congress has ruled the country, ultimately gain/loss credit will go to it.

NO matter what the critics of Jawaharlal Nehru's or any other Government say, but their commitment to democracy, secularism, social justice, independent foreign policy is unquestionable. It was the vision of Mahatma Gandhi and Nehru that helped lay a solid economic and secularly foundation for a nation that had just gained independence.

When India got Independence, there were very limited natural resources and 80% of Indians were poor and backwards. A vast majority of the people was living below the subsistence level. There was a problem of clean drinking water, proper sanitation, shelter, begging, slum areas and, in brief we can say, India was totally backward and uncared by the Britishers.

Early period of 1900-1947, tell the story of growth rate of Indian economy which was less than 1 per cent. After Independence i.e. 1947-64 annual growth rate was increase to 4.1 per cent, which was a great achievement. Indian growth rate again increased to 5.2 per cent in 1990-2002. The annual growth rate was around 8 per cent during the first decade of 21st century which shows India was heading towards advancement

Decade-wise reflection of India and economic indicators can be seen from the following figures.

Eco. Scene	1950-51	1960-61	1970-71	1980-81	1990-91	2000-2001	2009-10	2012-13
G.D.P	10036	17049	44382	136838	531814	1991982	6108903	9461979
Foodgrains (Million tons)	50.8	82	108.40	129.60	176.40	196.80	218.10	255.36
Cement	2.70	8	14.30	18.60	48.80	99.20	207.10	230.50
Electricity Generators KWH-billion (kwh-billion)	5	17	56	111	264	499	771	817
Birth rate	39.9	41.7	36.90	33.90	29.50	25.40	22.10	21.8(2012)
Death rate	27.4	22.8	14.90	12.50	9.8	8.40	7.2	7.1(2012)
Llfe expectancy rate	32.1	41.3	45.60	50.40	58.7	62.50	NA	66.1
Literacy rate	18.3	28.3	34.40	43.60	52.2	64.90	NA	66.1
No.of vehicles (million)	0.3	0.7	1.9	5.4	21.4	55.10	141.90	159.50

While analyzing the above data, it is apparent that in addition to G.D.P there was all around growth in every field. Construction material, Birth and death rate, Life Expectancy rate, Literacy Rate and No. of vehicles etc. These things speak the story of development of India.

Thus, the above era was full of events and challenges. To give a new life to the shattered economy, India initiated a process of development through Planning. In this context the First Five-Year Plan was started in the year 1951. The Plan took into consideration the necessity of implementation schemes of development initiated by the Government prior to commencement of the Plan as also the need to correct the mal-adjustments in the economy caused by war and Partition and after the General Election.

During the First Plan(1951-56) National Income was considerably increased 18%. In this plan, highest priority was given to Agriculture in view of heavy import of food grains and inflation.

Since Independence, India with leading population in the world, had been facing challenges of Food Security for poor people. There was a need to take an initiative to increase the Agricultural production. Taking this into consideration, the Agriculture promotion was initiated to increase the food production for feeding close to 33 crores people in the 1950s. It was the time when there was an acute shortage of food grains and India had to receive food under PL-480 agreement with United States. To overcome this problem, India targeted self-sufficient in food and launched various measures such as High Yielding variety seeds, improved fertilizers for Agricultural improvement. This improvement resulted in green revolution. From a mere 50 million tons(mt) of annual food grain production in 1950, India produced a record of 255.36 Mt food grains. Thus it was a significant jump and as a result production increased dramatically.

The objective of the Second Plan (1956-61) was to increase the national income, rapid industrialization with more emphasis on basic and heavy industries, provide more employment opportunities and get rid of inequalities in income and wealth and promote socialistic pattern of society.

At the end of the Second Plan, the national income was increased moderately to 20 per cent as against the target of 25%. Target growth was 4.5% but 4.2% was achieved. Heavy industries like the Durgapur, Bhilai and Rourkela steel plants were set up.

In the Third Plan (1961-66), the economy entered the take-off stage. Due to two wars - one with China in 1962 and the other with Pakistan in 1965, the period was not satisfactory and resources had to be diverted to defence. Throughout this Plan, there was drought, reduction in agricultural production and savings and investments. Targeted growth was 5.6% but 2.8% was achieved, which was on the lower side.

In view of the fact that due to failure of the Third Plan, the Government was forced to declare a Plan holiday. Three Annual Plans were started. More emphasis was given to agriculture production.

The Fourth Plan could be started in the year 1969. The main objective of this Plan was self-reliance, reduction in food import and industrial development.

Record food production on account of Green Revolution was noticed during the Plan. Target growth was 5.7%, but only 2.01% was achieved.

The Fifth Plan (1974-79) was started with the objective of eradication of poverty and to raise the standard of living of people who were living below the poverty line. The target of the Fifth Plan was to raise per capita consumption level. The target growth of 4.4% was achieved.

Correspondingly, the Sixth Plan was started in the year 1980. The main goal of the Plan was a significant step-up in the rate of growth of economy, technology, self-reliance, reduction in poverty and employment, regional inequalities, controlling of population and improvement of quality of life of people.

During this period the Indian economy made all-around progress and most of targets were achieved.

The Seventh Plan (1985-90) aimed at direct attack on the problems of poverty and unemployment and upgrading the technology. A satisfactory level of food grain production was achieved. Target growth rate was within the range.

The objectives of the Eighth Plan (1992-97) were generation of adequate employment to achieve near full employment level, process of fiscal reforms and economic reforms, increase the industrial growth rate, containment of population growth, eradication of illiteracy, safe drinking water and self-sufficiency in food. During this period 6.6% economic growth rate was achieved.

Growth with social justice was the aim of the Ninth Plan. Emphasis was on safe drinking water, primary education and empowerment to the woman.

The country was on the path of a planning model and it completed the Tenth and Eleventh Plans successfully with an increase in the GDP growth rate to 7.5% and 7.9% which was quite satisfactory.

The Twelfth Plan (2012-17) was started in the year 2012. The draft approach was approved by the NDC on 22nd October, 2011. More emphasis was laid on agricultural, rural development, roads, railways, health, skilled development, social inclusion, growth rate and reducing the Central Government deficit. The theme of the approach paper was faster and sustainable and more inclusive growth. It proposes a growth target of 8%.

TABLE SHOWING THE DETAIL OF GDP

Five years Plans	Period	GDP-Target	GDP Achieved
First	1951-56	na	na
Second	1956-61	4.5	4.21
Third	1961-66	5.6	2.72
Fourth	1969-74	5.7	2.05
Fifth	1974-79	4.4	4.83
Sixth	1980-85	5.2	5.54
Seventh	1985-90	5.0	6.02
Eighth	1992-97	5.6	6.68
Ninth	1997-02	6.5	5.5
Tenth	2002-07	8.0	7.7
Eleventh	2007-12	9.0	8
Twelfth	2012-17	8.0	na

Thus planning and its implementation were adopted by India more sincerely and got very cheering results.

During the above era, good and bad moments of the country can be summarized as under:

GOOD MOMENTS OF INDIA

ECONOMIC DEVELOPMENT

- The GDP of the country increased from Rs. 10,036 millions in 1950-51 to Rs. 94,61,979 in 2012-13. Here, the GDP, means Gross Domestic Product (GDP), is the broadest quantitative measure of a nation's total economic activity. More specifically, the GDP represents the monetary values of all goods and services produced within a nation's geographic borders over a specified period of time. The equation used to calculate GDP is as follows:

  GDP = Consumption + Government Expenditures + Investment+ Exports – Imports

  When the GDP declines for two consecutive quarters or more, by definition the Economy is in a recession. Meanwhile, when the GDP grows too quickly and fears of Inflation arise, the Government often attempts to stimulate the economy by raising interest rates.

  Thus, the GDP of the country is a matter of concern for economist and the Government. India's GDP is increasing which shows that India is going in the right direction. India has to maintain the GDP in future at idle level.

- Food production was enhanced to 255.36 million tons from 50.8 million tons which is more than five times.
- In this period, India had got a taste of the Green and White Revolutions also. Thus, India could be doing well in self-reliance as the major importance was given to the agriculture sector. During this time, India was able to export many produce to different countries as the Green Revolution was the result of hybrid seed and introduction of new farm machinery and equipment. These include cultivation by tractors instead of ox-drawn carts.
- The development of the country can also be judged by the production of cement and steel. The production of both the items has also been drastically increased which indicates that during this period construction activities have improved and enhanced.
- On 19th July, 1969, all private commercial banks whose deposit base was Rs. 50 crore or above, were nationalized by the Government of India. The main purpose of nationalization was that private commercial banks failed in catering to the credit needs of poor people
- Improvement in electricity generation is also the biggest achievement of the Government
- The above era may also be called as electrical revolution period. A number of dams were constructed on various rivers for generation of electricity. Some of the important dams are as under:
- Tehri Dam (Uttaranchal) was constructed in the year 2005. It is the highest dam in India and 8th highest dam in the world. The dam has the capacity for generation of 1000 megawatts of hydroelectricity.
- Bhakra Dam (Himachal Pradesh) is also the largest dam of India and highest gravity dam in the world. Its

construction was completed in 1963 with a capacity for generation of 1350 megawatts of hydroelectricity.

- Hirakund Dam (Odhisa), one of the longest dams in the world, was built across the Mahanadi. This dam was completed in the year 1957.

  In addition to the above, the Government of India has constructed various dams like Nagarjuna Sagar Dam (1974), Sardar Sarover Dam, Gujarat, and Pong Dam (1974) on the Beas river. There are scores of dams in every State which are helpful in the development of the country.
- The key achievement of this era was life expectancy rate which was improved from 32.6 years in 1951 to 66.1 in 2012. It shows that the Government has done to some extent satisfactory job in the field of health. A large number of hospitals and health centres have been opened in the public as well as private sectors.
- Birth, death and literacy rates have also been improved considerably.
- India conducted its first Nuclear Test on 18th May, 1974, at Pokhran under the leadership of Smt. Indira Gandhi.
- India conducted its second Nuclear Test on 11th May, 1998, Pokhran-II (Operation Shakti), under the leadership of Shri Atal Behari Vajpayee. Immediately after it the Prime Minister convened a press conference to declare India a full-fledged nuclear state
- In April, 1975, Aryabhata, first indigenously built Indian satellite, manufactured by ISRO, was launched from Russia. Its mission life was 17 years. The main purpose of this satellite was to gain experience in building and operating a satellite in space. Thereafter Insat-1, Insat-1D, Rohini and Apple satellite vehicles were launched

- Various industrial policies were launched in 1948, 1956, 1977, 1980 and 1991. The aim of New Industrial Policy, 1991, was to unshackle the Indian industry from bureaucratic control, to remove the restrictions of the FDI and to introduce liberalization with a view to integrating the Indian economy. In short, it may be termed as Abolition of Industrial Licensing, MRTP Act and lesser roller of public sector, etc.
- The then Congress Government initiated liberalization reforms in the year 1991. The same reforms were continued by other Governments and declared their intention of strengthening the reforms. No doubt, the credit of these reforms goes to Shri P.V. Narasimha Rao, Prime Minister of India, and Shri Manmohan Singh, Finance Minister of India, but behind the scene, the credit goes to the IMF. The IMF imposed a condition on India which we know today as liberalization, privatization and globalization.
- The Government of India started various employment generation programmes such as Swaran Jayanti Rozgar Yojana in 1997, Pradhan Mantri Gramodya Yojana-2000, Employment Assurance Scheme and Mahatma Gandhi Rural Employment Guarantee Act-2006.
- Niti Aayog, National Institution for Transforming India Aayog, was established on Ist January, 2015, that replaces the Planning Commission. Policy making think-tank was included in this institution. The function of this Aayog is to provide strategic and technical advice to the Central and State Governments.

SOCIAL ADVANCEMENT

- After Independence, India has experienced a rapid increase in the registered motor vehicles i.e. from 0.3 millions in 1951 to 159.5 millions as on 31st March, 2012. It is a sign to show that the standard of living of more and more people has increased.
- The Government of India passed the Untouchability Offences Act in 1955. The Act states that any person forcing the disabilities of untouchability can be sentenced to six months' imprisonment or a fine of Rs. 500 or both for his first offence. For every subsequent offence, the sentence will include both a term in jail as well as a fine. If considered necessary, the punishment can also be increased.
- It was a matter of pride when India won the first Cricket World Cup in the year 1983 under the captaincy of Kapil Dev.
- Bonded labour was a curse in India. In 1976, Parliament approved the Bill on abolishing bonded labour. Similarly, a law was enacted to curb child labour.
- It was a matter of pride moment for India when Mother Teresa got the Noble Peace Price in the year 1979.
- India entered the car era very fast when the first fleet of Maruti cars rolled out in India. The car revolution started from the year 1983.
- The Pradhan Mantri Jan-Dhan Yojana (PMJDY) is National Mission for Financial Inclusion to ensure access to financial services, namely banking/savings and deposit accounts, remittance, credit, insurance, pension in an affordable manner. An account can be opened in any bank branch or business correspondent (Bank Mitr) outlet. PMJDY accounts are being opened with zero balance.

However, if the account-holder wishes to get a cheque book, he/she will have to fulfill the minimum balance criterion.

Special benefits under PMJDY Scheme

- Interest on deposit
- Accidental insurance cover of Rs. 1.00 lakh
- No minimum balance required
- Life insurance cover of Rs. 30,000
- Easy transfer of money across India
- Beneficiaries of government schemes will get direct benefit transfer in these accounts
- After satisfactory operation of the account for 6 months, an overdraft facility will be permitted
- Access to pension, insurance products
- Accidental insurance cover, RuPay Debit Card must be used at least once in 45 days
- Overdraft facility up to Rs. 5,000 is available in only one account per household, preferably operated by a woman member of the household
- Similarly, the Pradhan Mantri Jeevan Jyoti Bima Yojana will offer a renewable one-year accidental death-cum-disability cover of Rs. 2 lakh to all savings bank account holders in the age group of 18-70 years at a premium of Rs. 12 per annum per subscriber
- Other social schemes such as Atal Pension Yojana and Pradhan Mantri Jeevan Jyoti Bima Yojana were also launched by the Government of India
- To promote gender equality and economic empowerment of women, the Government of India established India's first women bank, Bharatiya Mahila Bank, on 25th September, 2013

- The food-for-work programme was launched by the Government in the year 1977-78

POLITICAL AND TECHNOLOGY

- India successfully conducted 16 General Elections in the country from 1951 to 2015.
- The Government was successful in starting the first television service in India on 15th September, 1959, when All India Radio set up on an experimental basis television service in Delhi. This service was extended to Bombay and Amritsar in 1972
- The process of consolidation in the country was started in the year 1956. The States were reorganized on the basis of linguistic and aspirations of the people.
- Prime Minister Indira Gandhi announced the 20-Point Programme on 14th January, 1982. The aim of this programme was to increase production of food items, vegetables, develop IRD Programme, solve drinking water problem, improvement of slum areas, family planning, healthcare facilities, minimum wages for agricultural labour, rehabilitate bonded labour, housing for rural families and expand Public Distribution System.
- To strengthen the democracy and involve the youth in Government making, Parliament reduced the voting age from 21 years to 18 in the year 1988.
- Communal harmony has been dealt by India with greater tolerance
- The Government introduced Panchayati Raj in October 1959 to make the village bodies more powerful. Under this programme, all responsibilities and authority were

handed over to village people so that they may play active role in the development of villages

- Historic Simla Agreement between India and Pakistan was signed by the Government of India in 1972.
- The Government of India has been able to frame an independent foreign policy and interference by any other country has turned zero.

Tibetans in India

India has also dealt the problem of the Tibetan community in an excellent way. The settlement of the Tibetan community was also a great challenge. According to demographic survey of Tibetans living in exile, conducted by CTA Planning Commission in 2009, approximately 1,28,014 Tibetans lived outside, of them 94,203 lived in India. However, unconfirmed reports suggest that this figure may be around 300,000.

Tibetans' migration to India can be described in three separate stages. The first wave began when the 14th Dalai Lama fled Lhasa in the direction of India in the spring of 1959 when the Chinese People's Liberation Army (PLA) crushed an uprising of Tibetans against the Chinese Communist authorities; second and third waves were during the 1980s and 1990s. The main organization of the Tibetan Diaspora is the Central Administration of the 14th Dalai Lama based in McLeodganj in Dharamsala in India. These NGOs deal with cultural and social life of Diaspora and and promotion of political Tibetan independence. The credit of their peaceful settlement goes to India. India provided the Tibetans place, shelter, education, etc.

The government-in-exile of Tibetans functions from McLeodganj at Dharamsala in Himachal Pradesh which coordinates and monitors their political activities in India. In 1960, the Government of Mysore (Karnataka at that time) allotted nearly 3,000 acres of land in Mysore district in Karnataka where the first Tibetan settlement, other than Dharamsala, came into existence in 1961.

CURRENCY

After Independence, the British coinage was continued. The monetary system remained unchanged at one rupee consisting of 64 pice or 192 pies.

India introduced anna series on 15th August, 1950. This was the first coinage of the Republic of India. The King's portrait was replaced with the Ashoka's Lions capital. The monetary system was retained with one rupee consisting of 16 annas. Later in 1955, the Indian Coinage (Amendment) Act that came into force w.e.f. Ist April, 1957, introduced a decimal series. The rupee was now divided into 100 paise instead of 16 anna or 64 pice. The "Naya Paise" coins were minted in the denominations of 1, 2, 5, 10, 20 and 50 naye paise. From 1968 onward, the new coins were called just paise instead naye paise.

Date	Currency
1835	1 rupee=16 annas=64 paise
Ist April, 1957	1 rupee=100 naye paise
Ist June, 1964	1 rupee=100 paise

After this 1, 2 and 5-rupee notes were issued in the 1990s.

The credit of conversion of currency also goes to the Indian Government.

Despite the above achievements, the Government had also bad moments in the history which shocked India.

These are:

- Death of Father of the Nation Mahatma Gandhi on 30th January, 1948
- Indo-China war during the year 1962
- Death of angel of peace Jawaharlal Nehru on 27th May, 1964
- Indo-Pakistan wars in 1948, 1965 and 1971 and had to bear the burden to expenditure on Bangladesh refugees
- Death of Lal Bahadur Shastri on 11th January, 1966
- Numerous communal disturbances in the country
- Road rage incidents
- Anti-Sikh riot of 1984
- Terrorism in Jammu and Kashmir and Punjab

FUTURE DEVELOPMENT OF INDIA

Now the electoral outlook has been changed, the main opposition party, BJP, has got the opportunity to rule the country. Its first Prime Minister Atal Behari Vajpayee set various examples and his contribution to the country cannot be forgotten. Mr. Narendra Modi has also given "Make In India" dream and the time will tell in which direction the country will go. However, their dreams are immense which show vision for future.

India's development can be judged in three phases. The first phase is 1950-80. Though the development in this phase was sluggish, it was in a systematic way and plan. Despite various challenges and wars during this period, it may be termed as elementary period of development.

The second phase is from 1980 to 2010. During this phase, we entered into an expansion stage and reached from deprived technology to hi-tech technology. Somewhat there is all-round development i.e. in the education field, rise in standard of living of people, decrease in the number of BPL people, using of technology by common people also.This phase may be termed as Economic growth through liberalization and information technology

The third phase (2010-2047) may be termed as "Make In India" and digital India. Everybody wants that our country should be developed, clean and hi-tech. The Prime Minister of India had already taken certain initiatives in this regard.

Modi Government came with a new and fresh strength. People who are living in India or abroad have an immense faith upon him. Everybody is confident that the period of 2014-2047 is the name of India. New Government and future governments will leave no stone unturned to develop the country.

The hope of Prime Minister can be seen in his famous speech at the packed Madison square garden at USA with 20000 Non-Resident Indians. Modi said "that his big win in the Lok Sabha elections had come with a big responsibility for him which he would fulfill". Listing out India's advantages, the Prime Minister said "that its three strengths were democracy, demographic dividend in which 65 per cent of its population was under 35 years, and the demand for India because it was a huge market". Modi said, "My effort is to make development a mass movement. I am confident is that we will succeed."

This country is going to make rapid progress. Clearly with an eye on the younger generation, Modi said, "We will not do anything which will let you down.", "There is no reason to be disappointed. India will progress very fast and the skills of our youth will take India ahead." Recalling that Mahatma Gandhi turned the freedom struggle into a mass movement, Modi said at that time every Indian felt part of the crusade for the country's independence. It is his clear view is that governments along cannot bring development. At the maximum, the governments can launch only schemes. Attended by Indian-Americans from across the country and also from five provinces in Canada, this was the largest ever public reception to an Indian Prime Minister in America.

During this period, future of India is brilliant. There will be a good deal of dimensional increase in national wealth and per capita income. Due to Skill India, Digital India, Clean India, Rapid industrialization, reputation of India will increase in the eyes of world. Next phase is a phase of increased production, elimination of social and economic disadvantages, full utilization of resources.

We the people of India, will attain the highest position in the world due to rapid development.

Modi Government has already started worked in this direction Some of the important areas under:

SMART CITIES AND ATAL MISSION FOR REJUVENATION AND URBAN TRANSFORMATION (AMRUT)

A total of 98000 Crores rupees has been approved by Cabinet for the development of 100 smart cities and rejuvenation of 500 other cities.

For the smart cities Rs.48 thousand crores allocated while another Rs.50 thousand crores for AMRUT. The smart cities will be evaluated through criteria which are set by the Government of India. These cities will be equipped with modern infrastructure to lead a smart and decent life, clean and sustainable environment, which includes assured water, electricity supply, sanitation, solid waste management, E-Governance and safe and security of Citizen etc. The Government has already on the job and preliminary work has been done in this regard. This is the first footstep in the direction of Modern India.

COMPREHENSIVE PLAN TO CLEAN GANGA

The holy river Ganga has been facing serious threat due to discharge of increasing quantities of sewage, effluents and other pollution on account of industrialization and urbanizations. Thus there is an urgent need to ensure effective rejuvenation of the river Ganga and to maintain minimum ecological flows in the river Ganga. Though programme of clean Ganga has already been started by Shri Rajiv Gandhi, but now the Union Cabinet approved a massive 20000 crore revolutionary budget for Modi's pet Namami Gange Programme for the next 5 years. The Centre will now take over 100 per cent funding of various activities/ project under this programme.

SWACHH BHARAT MISSION\

The Swachh Bharat Mission (SBM) emanate from the vision of the Government contained in the address of The President of India in his address to the Joint Session of Parliament on 9th June 2014: "We must not tolerate the indignity of homes without toilets and public spaces littered with garbage. For ensuring hygiene, waste management and sanitation across the nation, a "Swachh Bharat Mission" will be launched. This will be our tribute to Mahatma Gandhi on his 150th birth anniversary to be celebrated in the year 2019" SBM is being implemented by the government for urban and rural areas respectively. The swachh Bharat Mission objective are".

1. Elimination of open defecation
2. Eradication of Manual Scavenging.
3. Modern and Scientific Municipal Solid Waste Management.

The Mission will be in force till 2nd October 2019 including conversion of insanitary latrines into pour-flush latrines, Community toilets, Public toilets, Solid waste Management and Public Awareness. By Public Toilets, it is implied that these are to be provided for the floating population / general public in places such as markets, train stations, tourist places, or other public areas where there are considerable number of people passing by. By Community toilets, it is implied that a shared facility provided by and for a group of residents or an entire settlement. Community toilet blocks are used primarily in low-income and/or informal settlements / slums, where space and/or land are constraints in providing a household toilet. The estimated cost of implementation of SBM (Urban) based on unit and per capita costs for its various components is Rs. 62,009 Crore. The Government of India share as per approved funding pattern amounts to Rs. 14,623 Crore. In addition, a minimum additional amount equivalent to 25% of GoI funding, amounting to Rs. 4,874 Crore shall be contributed by the States as States. The balance funds is proposed to be generated through Private Sector participation and other sources.

A clean India drive would be the best tribute to Mahatma Gandhi on his 150 birth anniversary in 2019, said Narinder Modi, Prime Minister of India. Now it is a National Movement and each of the office, school, colleges, Technical Institutions, Privates Sectors, Banks, Insurance Companies have participated in this cleanliness drive. This drive will have a magical result by 2019.

MAKE IN INDIA

Make in India is an important program of Modi Government with an aim to give the Indian economy global recongnition. Modi said "FDI" should be understood as "First Develop India" along with "Foreign Direct Investment."

He urged investors not to look at India merely as a market, but instead see it as an opportunity. He said investors from abroad need to create jobs and insisted upon that the faster people are pulled out of poverty and more employment means more purchasing power.

India is the only country in the world which offers the unique combination of democracy, demography, and demand. The new Government was taking initiatives for skill development to ensure that skilled manpower was available for manufacturing. Mood of gloom among India's business have been observed in the last few years, due to lack of clarity on policy issues. The Prime Minister gave the example of the new Government's initiative on self-certification of documents, and said this was illustrative of how the new Government trusted the citizens. The Prime Minister said trust is essential for investors to feel secure. He also emphasized the need for "effective" governance. The Prime Minister also unveiled the Make in India logo.

The effect of Make in India compaign will be that India will intend to manufacturing hub. There will be an increase in employment and poverty will be reduced. Balance of payment of the country will improve.

No doubt, Make in India is an ambitious project, but to get all the above benefits, the government will have to keep its house in order and work with full of devotion, sincerely and integrity.

NITI AAYOG TO REPLACE PLANNING COMMISSION

The Planning Commission was constituted on 15.3.1950 through a Government of India Resolution, and has served India well. India, however, has changed dramatically over the past 65 years and undergone a paradigm shift over the past six decades - politically, economically, socially, technologically as well as demographically.

The role of Government in national development has seen a parallel evolution. Keeping with these changing times, the Government of India has decided to set up NITI Aayog (National Institution for Transforming India), in place of the erstwhile Planning Commission, as a means to better serve the needs and aspirations of the people of India.

The new institution will be a catalyst to the developmental process; nurturing an overall enabling environment, through a holistic approach to development going beyond the limited sphere of the Public Sector and Government of India. This will be built on the foundations of:

An empowered role of States as equal partners in national development; operationalizing the principle of Cooperative Federalism.

A knowledge hub of internal as well as external resources; serving as a repository of good governance best practices, and a Think Tank offering domain knowledge as well as strategic expertise to all levels of government.

A collaborative platform facilitating Implementation;by monitoring progress, plugging gaps and bringing together the various Ministries at the Centre and in States, in the joint pursuit of developmental goals.

Thus in view of globalization, demographically, economically and advancement of technology, rejuvenation of Planning commission was needed.

In addition to the above, the following are also his key achievements:

Bringing Cooking Gas now under direct cash benefit transfer scheme.

Diesel prices de-regulated

Foreign equity cap raised in defence sector to 49 per cent and 74 per cent in case of technology transfer

FDI in Rail infrastructure allowed.

FDI in insurance sector raised to 49%.

More than 15 crores bank accounts opened under Jan Dhan Yojna scheme.

Mudra Bank launched with Rs.20000 crores to extend loan between Rs.50000 to Rs. 10 lacs to small enterprises.

Thus India has been projected as the country of future by National and international leaders. Our great scientist and visionary Ex-President of India, Dr A P J Abdul Kalam has rightly said, "A developed India by 2020 or even earlier, is not a dream. It need not be a mere vision in the minds of many Indians. It is mission we can all take up and succeed in the mission. A clear aim, knowledge, hard work and perseverance spell success. An ignited mind is the most powerful resources on earth. Our sweat will transform developing India into a developed nation".

Mission "Make India", "Skill India", "Swachh Bharat Mision" and "Digital India" is first step in this direction and Government eyes are on the completion of these mission.

CHAPTER 4

ROOTS OF PROBLEMS - POPULATION

It is a matter of great concern that world population has touched 7.33 billions in July 2015. The topmost TWO countries contributing to increase in the population are China and India

It is not only a burning topic of the world but a serious problem of our country also. With 18% of world population as on mid 2015, India is today the second largest populated country in the world. In 1991 India population was 84.63 crores with 43.92 crores males and 40.70 are females which have been increased today as 131 billion with 67.94 crores males and 63.15 crores females. The sex ratio of male is 108 as against 100 of females.

Though population explosion is a major problem being faced by several other countries too, with the world population estimated to reach between 10-12 billion by the beginning of the 2100, the problem is much more severe in India because of the increasing pressure on the limited resources of the country. With the growth of food grains not keeping pace with the increase in population during some years because of the unfavourable weather conditions, the specter of hunger hunts millions of households in the country.

As per the findings of Department of Economic and Social Affairs of United Nations, the world population reached 7.3 billion as of mid 2015. Out of which 60% population lives in Asia (4.4)billion, 16% in Africa (1.2billion),10% in Europe (738 million), 9% in Latin America.

Photo by Rajendra Sharma at Chandigarh on 1/12/2015.

China 1.4 billion and India 1.3 billion. remains in two largest countries of the world which contains 19% and 18% of the world population respectively. As per the figures available 50.4% of the world population is male and 49.6% are female.

About 26% populations of the world are under 15 years of age, 62% are 15-59 years and 12% are 60 or over. The population of group of 60 is increasing @3.26 per cent per years. The number of older persons are going to increase 2.10 billion in 2.50.

Though world population is growing slowly than in the recent past, yet as per estimates, it will reach 8.5 billions in 2030, and to increase further 9.7 billion in 2050 and 11.2 billion by 2100. There is an 80 per cent probability that the population of world will be between 8.4and 8.6 billion in 2030, between 9.4 and 10 billion in 2050 and between 10 and 12.5 billion in2100.

Sr.Ban ki Moon, Secretary General of UNO, said, "The world today has its largest generation of youth in history – 1.8 billions young people, mostly in developing countries – with enormous potential to help tackle the major challenges facing humanity. But too many are denied their rightful opportunities to get a quality education, find decent work, and participate in the political life of their societies. World Population Day is an opportunity to renew our commitment to help young people unleash progress across society. Action is urgently needed. Too many young people lack resources they need to lift themselves out of poverty. I am particularly concerned about adolescent girls who may face discrimination, sexual violence, early marriage and unwanted pregnancies. And even among those young people fortunate enough to receive university degrees, many find themselves without employment or stuck in low-wage, dead-end jobs."

Since India is the second largest country in contributing population after China, therefore, we cannot escape from our responsibilities. If population of any country is in order, everything is in order.

ANALYSIS OF INCREASE IN POPULATION

To Analysis the reasons of increase in population in India, we have to study the facts and figures of population growth in relation to the birth, death and literacy rates in India.

The population, which was 23.83 crore in 1901, increased to 121 crore i.e. 98 crore in 110 year with a growth rate of 407%. If the trend of increase in population will remain the same, the day is not far away when our all resources like wheat, sugar, vegetables, etc. will not be sufficient to distribute among the people. It is the time to control the population of India and to adopt the strict measures with the consent of Political as well as spiritual leaders

Tables 1 to III show the statistics which are used for analysis.

Population and its Growth, India: 1901-2011(TABLE-1)

	Population	Decadal growth		Change in decadal growth		Average annual exponential growth rate (percent)	Progressive growth rate over 1901 (percent)
		Absolute	Percent	Absolute	Percent		
1901	23,83,96,327		-	-	-	-	-
1911	25,20,93,390	1,36,97,063	5.75	-	-	0.56	5.75
1921	25,13,21,213	-7,22,177	(0.31)	-14469240	-6.05	-0.03	5.42
1931	27,89,77,238	2,76,56,025	11.00	28428202	11.31	1.04	17.02
1941	31,86,60,580	3,96,83,342	14.22	12027317	3.22	1.33	33.67
1951[1]	36,10,88,090	4,24,27,510	13.31	2744168	-0.91	1.25	51.47
1961[1]	43,92,34,771	7,81 ,46,681	21.64	35719171	8.33	1.96	84.25
1971	54,81,59,652	10,89,24,881	24.80[6]	30778200	3.16	2.20	129.94
1981[2]	68,33,29.097	13,51,69,445	24.66[6]	26244564	-0.14	2.22	186.64

1991[3]	84,64,21,039	16,30,91,942	23.87	27922497	17.12	2.16	255.05
2001[4]	1,02,87,37,436	18,23,16,397	21.54	19224455	10.54	1.97	331.52
2011[5]	1,21,01,93,422	18,14,55,986	17.64	-860411	-0.47	1.64	407.64

The table shows the decadal growth of population from 1901 to 2011. It shows that during 1901 to 1951, the population grew at 12.27 crore in 50 years with 51.46 per cent growth rate. The decadal growth is 5.75% in 1911, 0.31 in 1921, 11% in 1931, 14.22% in 1941 and 13.31% in 1951. This period may be termed as idle growth.

During 1961 to 2011 (the next 50 years), the population increased by 77.10 crore with 181.39% growth rate which is on very higher side. It was surprising that decadal growth of population increased from 13.31% in 1951 to 21.64% in 1961, 24.80% in 1971, 24.66% in 1981, 23.87% in 1991, 21.54% in 2001 and 17.64% in 2011. Thus, a trend of population explosion started after 1951.

Almost all States and Union Territories also show the same trend in increase of population after 1951. It is observed that consolidated annual growth rate of population in 2011 is 1.76%, whereas the States like Jammu and Kashmir, NCRT, Rajasthan, Uttar Pradesh, Bihar, Arunachal Pradesh, Jharkhand, Chhatisgarh, Madhya Pradesh, Daman & Diu, Dadar Nagar Haveli, Pondicherry and Andaman & Nicobar Islands registered a growth rate of more than 2% which is on very higher side, though in some States migration from Bangladesh may be the factor. India needs to launch an overall population awareness programme immediately.

We have no hesitation to record the appreciation for other States where population has not increased too much and they have major contribution to a decrease in the population of India.

TABLE III
REASONS OF INCREASING THE POPULATION FROM 1951 TO 2001

During this period, there was a rapid increase in the population. To analysis the reason, we have to study the birth and death rates of India since 1901.

Year	Crude Birth Rate	Crude Death rate	Natural growth rate
1901	45.8	44.4	0.14
1911	49.2	42.6	6.6
1921	48.1	47.2	0.9
1931	46.4	36.3	10.1
1941	45.2	31.2	14
1951	40.8	25.1	15.7
1961	41.7	22.8	18.9
1971	41.2	19.00	22.2
1981	33.9	12.5	21.4
1991	29.5	9.8	19.7
2001	25.4	8.4	17.0
2011	21.8	7.1	14.7
2012	21.6	7.0	14.6
2013	21.4	7.0	14.4

TABLE -IV
LITERACY RATE IN INDIA

Year	Crude literacy rate	Effective literacy rate
1901	5.35	NA (5.50)
1911	5.29	NA (6.00)
1921	7.16	NA (9.16)
1931	9.50	NA (11.00)
1941	16.10	NA (18.10)
1951	16.67	18.33
1961	24.02	28.30

1971	29.45	34.45
1981	36.23	43.57
1991	42.84	52.21
2001	54.51	64.83
2011	64.32	74.04

The crude literacy rate means "all population, including infants" and effective literacy means "population above 7 years"

ANALYSIS OF TABLES

While analyzing Table III and Table IV, it is understood that the main factors contributing to growth in population of India are:

- Increased birth rate
- Reduced mortality rate
- Increased literacy rates
- Medical technology

These factors are inter-related with population and it is a proven case in India. When initially literacy rate of any country improves, the result will be an increase in the birth rate and decrease in the death rate. This is due to medical technology improvement. Later on when it improves completely, then the birth and death rates will be highly decreased. This principle is applicable on population.

At a glance on the above table we shall find as under:

- Trends of population during 1901-1921 are almost equal. The same is the case with literacy rate. During this period, population was idle. This is the stage when population of country does not increase rapidly because there is neither any birth control measure nor any control on death. The literacy rate was 5% only. There is no medical advancement in the country. It is understood that when the death and birth rates are high, there will be a low literacy rate, low medical advancement, natural calamities, famines and epidemics. These are the signs of low standard of living and backwardness of a nation.

- Further, while analyzing Table III and Table IV, it is observed that there is considerable improvement in the birth rate from 45.8 (1901) to 21.8 (2011) and death rate from 44.40 (1901) to 7.1 (2011). The reason of this improvement is literacy rate. It is obvious that effective literacy rate in the year 1901 was 5.50 approximately which was highly improved in the year 2011 to 74.04.
- Contribution of the literacy rate is good achievement of the Government. Due to this, the country was successful in all-around activities like medical advancements. Zero rates of polio, malaria and T.B. are good examples to control the death rate.
- Now India is at the take-off stage or at breakeven points. The trend of decrease in the population has already been started and the literacy level is increasing day by day. I am sure, if the Government takes a proper care to educate the people who are below the poverty line, we can maintain a good level of decrease in population.

THE POPULATION OF INDIA IN 2047

The question arises what will be the trend of population in 2047. We can understand the trend with the following table where the literacy rate is more than 99%.

Name of Country	Literacy rate approx.	Birth rate	Annual growth as on date
Indonesia	99	17.76	1.40
Italy	99	09.06	0.6
Norway	99	10.80	1.0
Poland	99	09.96	-0.0
Russia	99	10.94	-0.0
Sweden	99	10.24	-0.8
United States	99	13.68	-0.9
India	74.4	21.8	1.77

These are the examples of a few countries. We can see the difference between India and other countries - surprising difference. On going through the trend of Table III, we can say we will get a literacy rate of 99% in the year 2047.

Similarly, if we analyse the above table, the projected population of India can be summarized as under:

PROJECTED POPULATION OF INDIA 2047

Year	Literacy rate	Projected literacy rate	Birth rate	Projected birth rate	Decadal growth %age	Population	Population projection
2011	74.4	NA	21.8	NA	17.70	121.00	NA
2021		84		19.00	13.00		137 millions
2031		94		17.00	09.00		150 millions
2041		99		13.00	05.00		158.00 millions
2047		99.5		0.9.00	0.200		161.00 millions

National Population Policy

The National Population Policy was announced in the year 2000. The policy took note of the fact that the growth in population was due to the large size of the population in the reproductive age, high fertility due to inadequate availability of contraception, high wanted fertility due to high infant mortality rate and most of the girls marrying below the age of 18. Some of the important objectives of the policy were as under:

- Address the unmet needs for basic reproductive and child health services, supplies and infrastructure.
- Make school education up to age 14 free and compulsory, and reduce dropout rate at primary and secondary school levels to below 20 per cent for both boys and girls.
- Reduce infant mortality rate to below 30 per 1000 live births.
- Reduce maternal mortality ratio to below 100 per 100,000 live births.
- Achieve universal immunization of children against all vaccine preventable diseases.
- Promote delayed marriage for girls, not earlier than 18 and preferably after 20 years of age.
- Achieve 80 per cent institutional deliveries and 100 per cent deliveries by trained persons.
- Achieve universal access to information/counseling and services for fertility regulation and contraception with a wide basket of choices.
- Achieve 100 per cent registration of births, deaths, marriages and pregnancies.
- Contain the spread of Acquired Immunodeficiency Syndrome (AIDS), and promote greater integration between the management of reproductive tract infections (RTIs) and sexually transmitted infections (STIs) and the National AIDS Control Organization.
- Prevent and control communicable diseases.

- Integrate Indian Systems of Medicine (ISM) in the provision of reproductive and child health services, and in reaching out to households.
- Promote vigorously the small family norm to achieve replacement levels of TFR.
- Bring about convergence in implementation of related social sector programmes so that family welfare becomes a people-centered programme.

MEASURE TO REDUCE POPULATION

Though the Government has made all out efforts to reduce the population, the achievements were below the standard rates. This may be due to the Emergency effect imposed by the Government of India in the year 1975.

Now it is the need of the hours to adopt on a war footing measures to reduce the population.

- Compulsory education to all and increase the rate of literacy rate to 94% up to the year 2021.
- War-footing publicity of the Family Planning measures in the media.
- Target to go one step above from projected table.
- To eradicate the problem of begging.
- To end child labour gravely.
- Registration of immediate marriages and comprehensive sex education.
- Removal of the notion, especially in the mind of members of the minority communities, that "God will feed me and my children".

- To improve the Family Planning programme with the political and religious support.
- Marriage age should be increased to 24 for girls and 26 for boys.
- Integrate lessons on population education in school and colleges.

People around the world must understand that overpopulation is a serious problem. At this juncture, we must inspire the people, to reduce birth rate below a two child average. Religion and population should not be linked with each other. As per my personal opinion, if we could achieve the target of literacy rate 94 per cent in 2021(as per above projected table), I am sure, there will be a remarkable reduction in the population. Government of India has a capacity and we can hope for the best.

CHAPTER 5

POVERTY

Poverty in India has remained in question since Independence. It is a curse for any country. To eliminate poverty from the world, the Food Agricultural Organization and the World Health Organisation pledge to make all out efforts to reduce substantially, before the next millennium, starvation, famine and hunger.

Photo by Rajendra Sharma, Panchkula on 23rd Nov.2015

The signs of poverty in one or other country are the same. Some of the signs of poverty may be listed as under:

- Basic needs of people are not being met. Basic needs are food, clothing and shelter. In other words, people live without any food security.
- Mass level of begging
- Mass level of people living in slums, near rivers, bus stands, temples and along railway tracks and lack basic sanitary latrines.
- Poorer have to struggle to find the means to eat three meals a day.
- These people have to migrate for 6-8 months every year, away from their home to work as laborers.
- Per capita income is very low

The question relating to estimation of poverty is a subject of discussion. It is very complex to draw a demarcation line between poor and non-poor persons. A line has to be drawn for method of such measurement. The Planning Commission has appointed various expert committees/task groups which have studied these aspects and each of the committee has different views.

An expert group under the chairmanship of Dr Y.K. Alag was constituted in India in July 1977 by the Planning Commission to look into the estimation of poverty. The task force submitted the report in January 1979. This task group estimated the minimum calorie consumption for rural and urban areas as 2400 and 2100. The minimum consumption expenditure estimated by the committee was Rs. 49.1 for rural and Rs. 56.1 for urban areas per capita per month.

Another expert group was constituted under the chairmanship of Late Shri D.T. Lakhadwala in September 1989 on the estimation of poverty line and to redefine the poverty line. This expert group submitted the report in July 1993 and was accepted by the Government in March 1997 as the basis for computing the official estimates of poverty in India.

As per the views of expert group, the poverty line serves as a cut-off line for separating the poor and non-poor, given the size of distribution of population by per capita consumer expenditure classes. This group recommended that the consumption expenditure should be calculated based on calorie consumption as earlier; (ii) state specific poverty lines should be constructed and these should be updated using the Consumer Price Index of Industrial Workers (CPI-IW) in urban areas and Consumer Price Index of Agricultural Labour (CPI-AL) in rural areas; and (iii) discontinuation of "scaling" of poverty estimates based on National Accounts Statistics.

The official estimate of poverty was derived by the Planning Commission using the Expert Group (Lakhadwala) methodology until January 2011. The poverty ratio (i.e. the percentage of people living below the poverty line) and the number of poor for different years at the national level estimated from the Expert Group (Lakhadwala) are as under:

Year	Poverty ratio Rural Urban	Total	No. of poor (Millions Rural Urban	Total
1973-74	56.40 49.90	54.90	261.30 60	321
1977-78	53.10 45.20	57.30	264.30 64.60	328.90
1987-88	39.10 38.20	38.90	231.90 75.20	307.10
1993-94	37.30 32.40	36.00	244.00 76.30	320.30
2004-05	28.30 25.70	27.50	220.90 80.00	301.70

This group calculated the total poverty ratio as 27.50 in India and the number of poor persons was 30.17 crore in the year 2004-2005.

Again, another expert group was constituted in December 2005 under the Chairmanship of Shri Suresh Tendulkar for changes in the existing procedures of official estimates. This group submitted its report in 2011. More or less, all-India poverty ratio is calculated in the same way as in the Lakhadwala expert group.

The Planning Commission released the data of poverty for 1993-94 and 2005 derived from the expert group (Tendulkar method) in January 2011.

Year	Poverty ratio Rural Urban	Total	No. of poor (Millions Rural Urban	Total
1993-94	50 31.8	45.30	328.60 74.50	403.70
2004-05	41.8 25.7	37.20	326.30 80.80	407.10
2009-10	33.8 20.90	29.80	278.20 76.50	354.70
2011-12	25.7 13.70	21.90	216.70 53.10	269.80

Thus, as per Tendulkar methodology the poverty line ratio was increased from 27.50 to 37.20 in 2004-05 and the same case was with the number of poor i.e. from 301.70 to 407.10.

DR C. RANGARAJAN REPORT

The Planning Commission constituted an Expert Committee under the Chairmanship of Dr. C. Rangarajan in June 2012 which submitted its report in June 2014. As the poverty line defined by the Tendulkar Committee did not reflect the changing times and aspirations of the people, changes in the structure of economy as well as in people's prospective, the Planning Commission directed the committee to suggest a methodology for measurement of poverty with reference to fixation of the poverty line in terms of consumption of basket and to review alternative method of estimation of poverty.

After going out to the National Sample Surveys, the expert group is of the considered view that the consumption basket should contain a food and non-food components.

The various studies conducted by this group set up the average calorie requirement as 2155 kcpl per capita per day in rural areas and 2090 in urban areas. Earlier, this was fixed at 2400 and 2100 calories. This change was the outcome of change in the population structure.

As regard the monthly per capita expenditure, which constitutes the new poverty line basket separately in rural and urban areas, is Rs. 972 for rural area and Rs. 1,407 for urban areas. The total monthly expenditure of a five-member family comes to Rs. 4,860 in rural areas and Rs. 7,035 in urban areas at the 2011-12 prices. Poverty estimation as per the Rangarajan Committee is as per under noted table:

Year	Poverty ratio Rural Urban	Total	No. of poor (Millions Rural Urban	Total
2009-10	39.60 35.10	38.20	325.90 128.70	454.60
2011-12	30.90 26.40	29.50	260.5 102.40	363.00

Thus, the aggregate poverty ratio is estimated from the proposed population of the year at 30.90 for rural areas and 26.40 for urban areas. The aggregate ratio is 29.50.

As per the Rangarajan Committee report, the number of poor persons in the country is 26.05 crore in rural areas and 10.24

crore in urban areas. The total number of people living below the poverty line in India is 36.29 crore.

From the above analysis, we can conclude that as per the latest available figures, the total number of persons below the poverty line in India is 36.29 crore. Most of these people have per capita income per day of Rs. 32 for rural and Rs. 49 for urban areas.

Now the issue arises whether the above amount of Rs. 160 is sufficient to pull on a family of five. The apparent answer cannot be given. However, this is my opinion that if an individual who is homeless, living in a slum and is a seasonal employee can pull on his family with this amount. This is the reason why he has been kept below the poverty line. The question is what the Government has done to uplift such type of people.

Before going through the achievements and failures of the Government, it is important to know the causes of poverty. The main causes which need not more elaboration are over population, reduction in food production, lack of will power of poor persons to lift themselves, lack of will power of the Government to alleviate poverty from the country, rampant corruption, political and social factors and industrial development, poor agriculture and industrial growth and illiteracy.

If we go through the post-Independence era, we will find that the Government has done a lot to improve the standard of living of poor persons. I specially appreciate the Governments of Kerala, Punjab, Haryana, Himachal Pradesh, Jammu & Kashmir and Goa where the people under the poverty line are fewer compared to other States. On the other hand, the States like Bihar, Uttar Pradesh, Karnataka, Madhya Pradesh, Odhisa and Jharkhand have a very higher poverty ratio i.e. more than 30% of their population. The main issue is when some States have been able to control the poverty, why not others.

It will be appropriate to compare the Kerala model of population with Uttar Pradesh and Bihar. In 1951 Uttar Pradesh and Bihar population was 602.74 lakh and 290.95 lakh which was increased to 1995.81 lakh and 1038.46 lakh, respectively, whereas the literacy rate was too lower than Kerala, resulting in an increase in poverty in such states. Still their literacy rates are 69.72 and 63.82 per cent against the Kerala's rate of 93.91% in 2011.

It does not mean that our Government has not done any work in this direction. If we go through the Five-Year Plans, we will find that the Government is serious to remove poverty from the country.

British rulers gave India a shattered economy where everything was in poor state and it was one of the series of challenges to alleviate poverty. The ultimate objective of development in India since Independence has been the abolition of poverty and social backwardness. Despite several weaknesses, anti-poverty programmes have played an important role in alleviation of poverty and unemployment.

The achievements and failures of the Government in this direction can be enumerated as below:

The Integrated Rural Development (IRDP) Programme was launched by the Government of India in the year 1978-79. The purpose of this programme was to raise the standard of living of the Below Poverty Line families, especially in rural areas. The target group consists largely of small and marginal farmers, agricultural labourers and rural artisans living below the poverty line. The pattern of subsidy is 25 per cent for small farmers, 33-1/3 per cent for marginal farmers, agricultural labourers and rural artisans and 50 per cent for Scheduled Caste/Scheduled Tribe families and physically handicapped persons. The ceiling for subsidy is Rs. 6,000 for each Scheduled Caste/Scheduled Tribe family and the physically handicapped; for others, it is Rs. 4,000 in non-DPAP/non-DDP areas and Rs. 5,000 in DPAP and DDP areas. Within the target group, there is an assured coverage of 50 per cent for Scheduled Castes and Scheduled Tribes, 40 per cent for women and 3 per cent for the physically handicapped. Priority in assistance is also given to the families belonging to the assignees of ceiling surplus land, Green-Card holders covered under the Family Welfare Programme and freed bonded labourers. The District Rural Development Agency was responsible for implementation of the IRDP. It was the largest programme of the Sixth Five-Year Plan for alleviation of property. It is a centrally sponsored scheme and is shared on 50:50 basis by the Centre and the States. While evaluating the scheme, experts and the Government have the views that some poor people have made moderate gain and about 15% beneficiaries could cross the poverty line. This step shows that the Government was serious to alleviate the poverty.

The next component of the IRDP is to provide training to rural youth for self-employment. The main purpose of this scheme is to provide technical and basic managerial skills to the rural youth below the poverty line. During the 8th Five-Year Plan period, 1,528 million youth were trained. The experts evaluated that youth did not utilize the knowledge gained under the programme.

In July 1992, the Ministry concerned also launched a scheme and supplied a kit of hand tools to crafts persons within a financial ceiling of Rs. 2,000. Under this scheme, artisans had to bear only

10 per cent of the cost, while the Government provided the rest as subsidy. A good number of tool kits were provided to rural artisans. The rural artisans are well versed with the scheme.

Despite all the faults, the IRDP is a significant series for poverty alleviation in the Ninth Five-Year Plan.

The National Rural Employment Guarantee Act 2005 (No. 42), now named as MGNREGA, received the assent of the President of India on 5th September, 2005. The purpose of the Act is to provide enhancement of livelihood securities of the households in rural areas by providing at least 100 days of guaranteed waged employment in every financial year to every household whose adult members volunteer to do unskilled manual work. MGNREGA is the first-ever Act/law internationally that guarantees waged employment in rural area and it is a symbol of the Rural Development and Panchayati Raj Institutions.

The main points of the scheme are as under:

- All adult members of a rural household willing to do unskilled manual work have the right to demand employment. Such a household will have to apply for registration to the Gram Panchayat
- After verification, the Gram Panchayat will issue a Job Card
- Job-Card holder can apply for work to the Gram Panchayat which will issue him receipt.
- If any applicant is not provided such employment within 15 days of receipt of his application, he shall be entitled to an unemployment allowance in accordance with the guidelines framed in the Act.
- At least one-third of the workers should be women

- Creche, drinking water and First Aid will be provided at worksites.
- The implementing and monitoring authorities will be the Central Employment Guarantee Council and the State Employment Guarantee Council.
- The panchayats at the district, intermediate and village levels shall be the principal authorities for planning and implementation of the scheme.
- The Central Government will bear the 100 per cent wage cost of unskilled labour and 75 per cent of the material cost, including the wages of skilled and semi-skilled workers.
- The Gram Panchayat shall be responsible for identification of projects and social audit of all the projects under the scheme taken up by the Gram Panchayats.
- Provision and execution of work is provided within a 5-kilometres (kms) radius of the village. In case, work is provided beyond 5 kms, 10 per cent extra wages are payable to meet the additional transportation and living expenses.
- Contractors and use of labour displacing machinery are prohibited.
- Payment of wages has to be done on a weekly basis and not beyond a fortnight in any case.
- Payment of wages is mandatorily done through bank/post office beneficiary accounts
- The work undertaken through MGNREGA gives priority to activities related to water harvesting, groundwater recharge, drought-proofing, as also the problem of floods
- Grievance procedure formulated.

PERFORMANCE OF MGNREGA

STORY OF MGNREGA SUCCESS

Description	2006-07	2007-2008	2008-09	2009-10	2010-11	2011-12	Consolidated results
No. of Distt.	200	330	615	619	626	626	626
Employment provided to householders	2.10 cr.	3.39 cr	4.51 cr	5.26cr	5.49 cr	5.04 cr	25.79 Cr
Budget outlays in crore	11300	12000	30000	39100	40100	40000	172500 cr
Expenditure	8823	15856	27250	37905	39377	37548	166759
Person days of employment	90.5	143.59	216.32	283.59	257.15	211.41	1202.11
Average wage rate per day	65	75	84	90	100	117	

The programme was started in February 2006 in 200 districts of India. It was spread to 330 districts in the first year of the Eleventh Plan (2007-08) and to the entire country, extended to 626 districts, up to 2011-2012. The employment provided to household through this programme in the very first year i.e. in 2006-2007 was 2.10 crore which was increased to 5.49 crore in 2010-2011.The total employment generated in six years is more than 25 crore. Likewise a Budget outlay of Rs. 11,300 crore was kept in 2006-2007 which was increased to Rs. 40,000 crore in 2011-2012. Thus, the total Budget outlay provided by the Government of India over the last six year was Rs. 1,72,000 crore. MGNREGA has generated more than 1,200 crore person days of work at a total expenditure of over Rs. 1,66,760 crore. Nearly 10 crore bank/post office accounts of poorest people have been opened and around 80 per cent of MGNREGA payments are made through this route, an unprecedented step in the direction of financial inclusion.

While analyzing the data of different States, it is observed that there are lots of States where MGNREGA has registered a very good outcome, whereas in some other States performance is not adequate. The reasons may be political or administrative. Whatsoever may be the reason, the intention of the Government is very understandable i.e. to alleviate poverty and unemployment.

A recent example is that the Union Cabinet on 15th September, 2015, approved 150 days' employment per household under the Mahatma Gandhi National Rural Employment Guarantee Act (MGNREGA) in the drought-hit areas of the country. A decision in this regard was taken by a Union Cabinet meeting chaired by Prime Minister Narendra Modi in New Delhi. Additional 50 days' of unskilled manual work under the MGNREGA scheme will benefit people in drought-hit areas which are facing monsoon deficit, affecting kharif crops and rural income. The move will enable the State Governments to provide additional waged employment to the rural poor from the present 100 days in drought and natural calamities affected States.

In addition to the above, the Government of India has launched various different types of schemes in different years which can be briefly stated as below:

Pradhan Mantri Gramodya Yojana (PMGY)

The Pradhan Mantri Gramodya Yojana (PMGY) was launched in 2000-2001 in all States and Union Territories (UTs) in order to achieve the objective of sustainable human development at the village level. The PMGY initially had five components viz primary health, primary education, rural shelter, rural drinking water and nutrition.

Swarnajayanti Gram Swarozgar Yojana (SGSY)

After a review and restructuring of the erstwhile Integrated Rural Development Programme and allied schemes, the Swarnajayanti Gram Swarozgar Yojana (SGSY) was launched in April 1999. The objective of the SGSY is to bring the assisted Swarozgaris above the poverty line by providing them income-generating assets through bank credit and Government subsidy. Since its inception and up to April 2004, a total allocation of Rs 6,734 crore was made available by the Centre and the States. An amount of Rs. 4,980 crore has been utilized up to April 2004, benefiting 45.67 lakh Swarozgaris. Thus, it can be termed as credit-sum-subsidy programme.

Sampoorna Grameen Rozgar Yojana (SGRY)

The Sampoorna Grameen Rozgar Yojana (SGRY) was launched in September 2001, by merging the ongoing schemes of the Jawahar Gram Samridhi Yojana (JGSY) and the Employment Assurance Scheme (EAS). The objective of the programme is to provide additional waged employment in the rural areas as also food security along with the creation of durable community, social and economic infrastructure in rural areas. The SGRY is open to all rural poor who are in need of waged employment and desire to do manual and unskilled work in and around the village/habitat. The scheme is implemented through the Panchayati Raj Institutions. The scheme envisages generation of 100 crore man-days of employment in a year. The cost of each component of the programme is shared by the Centre and the States in the ratio of 75:25. During the year 2003-04 an amount of Rs. 4,121 crore as cash component and 49.97 lakh tons of food grain were released to the States/UTs and 76.45 crore man-days (provisional) have been generated as reported by the States/UTs. Under the special component of the SGRY, 65.84 lakh tons of food grains have been released to 12 calamity affected States during 2003-04.

Rural Housing Schemes

The Indira Awaas Yojana (IAY) aims at providing dwelling units, free of cost, to the poor families of the Scheduled Castes (SCs), Scheduled Tribes (STs), freed bonded laborers and also the non-SC/ST persons Below Poverty Line (BPL) in the rural areas.

Food Security Programme

The World Food Summit of 1996 defined food security as existing "when all people at all times have access to sufficient, safe, nutritious food to maintain a healthy and active life. Food security is built on three pillars:

- Food availability: Sufficient quantities of food available on a consistent basis.
- Food access: Having sufficient resources to obtain appropriate foods for a nutritious diet.
- Food use: Appropriate use based on knowledge of basic nutrition and care as well as adequate water and sanitation.

Food security is a complex sustainable development issue, linked to health through malnutrition, but also to sustainable economic development, environment and trade. There is a great deal of debate around food security with some arguing that:

- There is enough food in the world to feed everyone adequately; the problem is distribution.

- Future food needs can or cannot be met by current levels of production.
- National food security is paramount or no longer necessary because of global trade.
- Globalization may or may not lead to the persistence of food insecurity and poverty in rural communities.

India has done a lot in this direction. Volume II of the Planning Commission states, "At the time of Independence the country faced two major nutritional problems; one was the threat of famine and acute starvation due to lack of national and regional food security systems; and the other was chronic under-nutrition due to low dietary intake because of lack of purchasing power among the poorer segments of the population.

One of the first efforts of the country was to build up a food security system to ensure that the threat of famine no longer stalks the country. Investment in agriculture and the Green Revolution have ensured that the food production has kept pace with the population growth and by and large India remained self-sufficient in food. Establishment of adequate buffer stocks has ensured availability of food stuff within affordable cost even during the times of drought. The food-for-work programme and employment assurance scheme are aimed at improving household food availability in Below Poverty Line (BPL) families, especially in seasons when the employment and food availability in rural areas are low. To some extent these measures have helped in the improvement in the household food availability but the problem of equitable distribution of available food and need-based intra-familial distribution of food persisted.

Public Distribution System (PDS) & Targeted Public Distribution Scheme

The purpose of this programme was to provide food grains at affordable prices to consumers and price support to farmers. This system played a vital role in improving the availability of food to population living in most remote, tribal and drought-prone regions. This PDS network expanded in 1970s and 1980s after the Green Revolution. To strengthen the programme, the Targeted Public Distribution System (TPDS) was introduced on June 1, 1997. The TPDS envisaged that the Below Poverty Line (BPL) population would be identified in every State and every BPL family would be entitled to a certain quantity of food grains at specially subsidized prices. The BPL population was offered food grains at half the economic cost.

Thus, the TPDS intends to target the subsidized provision of food grains to the "poor in all areas". The guidelines for the implementation of the TPDS were issued by the Ministry of Consumers Affairs, Food & Public Distribution in 1997. The TPDS proposed to issue 10 kg of food grains per BPL family (revised to 20 kg w.e.f. April, 2000) at specially subsidized rates.

FINANCIAL INCLUSION SCHEME

The Rangarajan Committee submitted its report on Financial Inclusion in January 2008. According to it, "Financial Inclusion may be defined as the process of ensuring access to financial services and timely and adequate credit where needed by vulnerable groups such as weaker sections and low-income groups at an affordable cost." As much as 51.4% of farmer households are financially excluded from both formal and informal sources of credit. Of the total farmer households, only 27% access formal sources of credit; one-third of this group also borrows from non-formal sources. Overall, 73% of farmer households have no access to formal source of credit. The objective of Financial Inclusion is to extend the scope of activities of the organized financial system to include within its ambit people with low income. Through graduated credit, the attempt must be to lift the poor from one level to another so that they come out of poverty.

Recently, the Government of India has launched the Pradhan Mantri Jan Dhan Yojana which is the biggest Financial Inclusion in the world. The scheme was announced by Prime Minister of India Narendra Modi on 15th August, 2014, and its mega launch was done by him on 28th August, 2014.

The purpose of this scheme is to remove financial untouchability and provide better economic equality. Under this scheme, every Indian family will be enrolled in a bank for opening a zero-balance account. Opening a bank account will be the first step to eradicate poverty and financial untouchability. More than 17.74 crore bank accounts have been opened and people have deposited more than Rs. 22,000 crore in these accounts.

The scheme has been started with a target to provide universal access to banking facilities starting with basic savings bank account with an overdraft up to Rs. 5,000, subject to satisfactory operation in the account for six months and RuPay debit card with inbuilt accident insurance cover of Rs. 1 lakh.

The Pradhan Mantri Suraksha Bima Yojana and the Jeevan Jyoti Bima Yojana are also launched for accidental insurance worth Rs. 2 lakh at just Rs. 12 p.a. from General Insurance and Life Insurance cover worth Rs. 2 lakh at just Rs. 330 p.a., respectively.

Hence, every Government, Congress, BJP, UPA and Janata Party, had made no stone unturned to eradicate poverty from the nation.

FUTURE OF POVERTY IN INDIA

The question is whether India will get a zero-poverty rate or not. If yes, then in which year. On the issue of poverty, Mr. Kaushik Basu, Senior Vice-President and Chief Economist, World Bank Group, said, "It is shocking to have a poverty line as low as $1.25 per day. It is even more shocking that 1/7th of the world's population lives below this line. The levels of inequality and poverty that prevail in the world today are totally unacceptable. This year's Global Monitoring Report, which brings together in one volume a statistical picture of where the world stands in terms of the World Bank Group's goals, is essential fodder for anyone wishing to take on these major challenges of our time."

The World Bank has projected the Global Monitoring Report, 2014/2015: Ending poverty and sharing prosperity introduce the WBG's twin goals and present the first account of the challenge of ending extreme poverty and promoting shared prosperity. The first goal is to essentially end extreme poverty by reducing the share of people living on less than $1.25 a day to less than 3 per cent of the global population by 2030.

The expert group study shows that India's poverty ratio is 29.50% and about 363 millions people are living below the poverty line. If we go through pre-Independence era, we shall find that the poverty ratio was more than 70%. During the post-Independence era, India made serious efforts and brought the poverty ratio to the extent of 29.50%.

The World Bank has set a target to bring the poverty ratio at the rate of 3% by 2030 in South Asia. The completion of this task is not so easy unless and until wholehearted efforts are made in this direction. If full efforts are made to control the population, then projected population must be around 1500 millions in 2030 and after calculating 3% poverty ratio, the total number of the poor comes to 4.50 crore which will be more than acceptable. To get 3% poverty ratio, India has to set the following targets:

- Reliable data of the Below Poverty Line people
- To control the population and increase the literacy rate
- Compulsory education to all
- Eradicate the menace of begging
- High economic growth rate
- Financial Inclusion in reality
- Implementation of self-employment programmes more vigorously
- Improvement in slum areas
- To identify the BPL people and to create employment opportunities for them
- Right to food to every person

Despite various constraints of resources, in the post-Independence era, the Government of India has taken various measures to eliminate poverty and to some extent it is victorious. Thus, it is logical that still near 300 million people live in extreme poverty in India and if India is on the development path and motivation to the poorest of the people under the dynamic and determination of leadership, there is no reason why we cannot complete the remarkable and revolutionary target of 3% by 2030 framed by the World Health Organization.

CHAPTER 6

CORRUPTION

Corruption is a gigantic problem of the world. It is a complex phenomenon. The roots of corruption are very deep. It is in the blood of greedy bureaucrats, political community and individuals. It is not a new phenomenon. It has existed since old civilizations. The corruption is a measurement of one's integrity. The word integrity denotes as –Honesty, genuineness and a man of sound principle. Honesty and integrity is an essential attribute of welfare states.

The question is, "Why it is a complex issue". It can be explained with the following example as the corrupt people have an aptitude to complaint falsely against an honest person also. In such cases sometimes honest man feel discouraged due to corrupt society.

There are numerous examples of this. But one of the tested examples is that one day a person received a call from one of the CEOs of a reputed company for medical insurance of his family. This insurance was through a bank. He replied politely, "Send so and so much premium through the bank". He sent the premium and the company had underwritten the same. There was a gap of around 90 days of the previous policy. After a few days, he lodged the claim to the TPA (third-party administrator). The

TPA straightway told him that the claim is not payable. Then he sent one of his juniors to the office and it was told by the office that it could not be paid as it was against the terms and conditions of the policy.

Though that CEO never came to the office either for insurance or for enquiry, he (may be his junior) wrote a letter to the company and to various unions that so and so person was demanding money for settlement of the claim. He attempted to pressurize the whole of the company in wrongful manner. He talked to him on the telephone, "Sir, why are you making wrong allegation against me."

The department held an inquiry and found that his allegation was baseless. In the meantime, he also complained to the Ombudsman for settlement of the claim. Since the label of honesty in the department was with a person, therefore, the dealing team went to the Ombudsman office to defend the case.

It is pertinent to mention here that he saw that person first time in the office of the Ombudsman. There was no limit of surprise for him that he repeated the allegation in front of him.

He did not know he was also there. Worthy Ombudsman asked him to explain the whole thing? He told him, "Sir, first listen the history of the case, reply of his allegation will be given later." He picked up a piece of paper from the file and handed it over to the worthy Ombudsman. "As per the paper, the person concerned had been admitted to the hospital prior to insurance." It was clear from the paper that he tried to cheat the company.

The team from the Ombudsman's office took serious view of it and dismissed his complaint. This was the complaint which troubled him for at least two months. Who is responsible for bad name to him.

Here it is not a matter of discussion whether the claim is payable or not, the question is that a wrong allegation can also be leveled against the honest man. Whenever, we deal with the alleged persons, we should see to it that the honest man should not be hurt in any way. Thus, why is it a very complex issue.

Corruption can be characterized as under:

- A client pays a bribe to government official or any organization in order to get a government tender, licence or favour.
- A government official takes advantage of his or her position to favour a family member or any near or dear one for a job or tender contract. This is commonly called nepotism.
- A police official solicits a bribe or a member of the public offers one in order to escape lawful punishment.
- Favour to any criminal or granting bail by judiciary.
- For granting loan to the client, demanding bribe by bank officer.
- Provide low-priced type of material to Government department other than specified.
- Using of D-grade material for construction by the contractor and, in turn, offers something to Government official.

These types of feature of corruption are also found in the Income Tax Department, Health Department, Judiciary i.e. lower courts and High Court, PWD, etc.

These are the only examples. Think any field, you will find corruption and corruption is everywhere, especially in South Asia.

DEFINITION

In my opinion "corruption may be defined as disruption of work by any official or officials, individuals, politicians or any other institution for getting wrongful gains and, in turn, to get their demand met by generous unwarranted favour to them. Both the parties i.e. one who pay the obsession i.e. in any kind of cash or gifts or donation and he who accepts the same, come under the purview of corruption".

The World Bank settled on a straightforward definition - ***the abuse of public office for private gain***. This definition is not original but it was chosen because it is concise and broad enough to include most forms of corruption that the bank encounters as well as being widely used in the literature.

Most newspapers of each and every country, except a few, are full of corruption news. Take an example of the USA, the USSR, China, Pakistan, Bangladesh, Lanka and England, etc. We shall find that no country is free from this iniquity. There must be variation in degree, percentage, but as far as its quality and magnitude are concerned, there is no disparity.

MEASUREMENT OF CORRUPTION

It is very difficult to measure the level of corruption in any country. The best-known indicator of measurement of national corruption is Corruption Perception Index (CPI) prepared by Transparency International. According to them, corruption caused due to bribery, abuse of power and unethical dealings continue to ravage nations around the world. Denmark retained its position as the least corrupt country in 2014 with a score of 92, while Somalia occupied the last place, scoring just 8. In India's neighbourhood, China moved to 100th place, down from 80th last year, while Pakistan and Nepal share the 126th position. Bangladesh was 145th and Bhutan 30th in the ranking. Sri Lanka was ranked 85th with India. Afghanistan was at a bleak 172. According to the Corruption Perception Index (CPI) report by the TII, "The CPI score for India increased by 2 points in 2014 from its 2013 score, helping India improve its rank to 85 in 2014 from 94 in 2013." India's score stood at 38 as compared to 36 last year.

The improvement in the CPI for India was driven primarily by two data sources — from the World Economic Forum and the World Justice Projects (WJP) index. "A score increase on WEF suggested businesses in India were viewing the environment favourably with regards to their perception of corruption and bribery in the country."

The WJP score also went up reflecting the perceptions of public sector corruption coming down slightly in India.

CORRUPTION PERCEPTION INDEX – 2014

		Score		Rank			
Country	ISO Codes	CPI 2014	CPI 2013	Rank 2014	Rank 2013	Rank 2012	Delta Rank (2013-2014)
Denmark	DNK	92	91	1	1	1	0
New Zealand	NZL	91	91	2	1	1	-1
Finland	FIN	89	89	3	3	1	0
Sweden	SWE	87	89	4	3	4	-1
Norway	NOR	86	86	5	5	7	0
Switzerland	CHE	86	85	5	7	6	2

Singapore	SGP	84	86	7	5	5	-2
Netherlands	NLD	83	83	8	8	9	0
Luxembourg	LUX	82	80	9	11	12	2
Canada	CAN	81	81	10	9	9	-1
Australia	AUS	80	81	11	9	7	-2
Germany	DEU	79	78	12	12	13	0
Iceland	ISL	79	78	12	12	11	0
United Kingdom	GBR	78	76	14	14	17	0
Belgium	BEL	76	75	15	15	16	0
Japan	JPN	76	74	15	18	17	3
Barbados	BRB	74	75	17	15	15	-2
Hong Kong	HKG	74	75	17	15	14	-2
Ireland	IRL	74	72	17	21	25	4
United States of America	USA	74	73	17	19	19	2
Chile	CHL	73	71	21	22	20	1
Uruguay	URY	73	73	21	19	20	-2
Austria	AUT	72	69	23	26	25	3
Bahamas	BHS	71	71	24	22	22	-2
United Arab Emirates	ARE	70	69	25	26	27	1
Estonia	EST	69	68	26	28	32	2
France	FRA	69	71	26	22	22	-4
Qatar	QAT	69	68	26	28	27	2
Saint Vincent and the Grenadines	VCT	67	62	29	33	36	4
Bhutan	BTN	65	63	30	31	33	1
Botswana	BWA	63	64	31	30	30	-1
Cyprus	CYP	63	63	31	31	29	0
Portugal	PRT	63	62	31	33	33	2
Puerto Rico	PRI	63	62	31	33	33	2
Poland	POL	61	60	35	38	41	3

Taiwan	TWN	61	61	35	36	37	1
Israel	ISR	60	61	37	36	39	-1
Spain	ESP	60	59	37	40	30	3
Dominica	DMA	58	58	39	41	41	2
Lithuania	LTU	58	57	39	43	48	4
Slovenia	SVN	58	57	39	43	37	4
Cape Verde	CPV	57	58	42	41	39	-1
Korea (South)	KOR	55	55	43	46	45	3
Latvia	LVA	55	53	43	49	54	6
Malta	MLT	55	56	43	45	43	2
Seychelles	SYC	55	54	43	47	51	4
Costa Rica	CRI	54	53	47	49	48	2
Hungary	HUN	54	54	47	47	46	0
Mauritius	MUS	54	52	47	52	43	5
Georgia	GEO	52	49	50	55	51	5
Malaysia	MYS	52	50	50	53	54	3
Samoa	WSM	52	#N/A	50	#N/A	#N/A	#N/A
Czech Republic	CZE	51	48	53	57	54	4
Slovakia	SVK	50	47	54	61	62	7
Bahrain	BHR	49	48	55	57	53	2
Jordan	JOR	49	45	55	66	58	11
Lesotho	LSO	49	49	55	55	64	0
Namibia	NAM	49	48	55	57	58	2
Rwanda	RWA	49	53	55	49	50	-6
Saudi Arabia	SAU	49	46	55	63	66	8
Croatia	HRV	48	48	61	57	62	-4
Ghana	GHA	48	46	61	63	64	2
Cuba	CUB	46	46	63	63	58	0
Oman	OMN	45	47	64	61	61	-3
The FYR of Macedonia	MKD	45	44	64	67	69	3
Turkey	TUR	45	50	64	53	54	-11

Kuwait	KWT	44	43	67	69	66	2
South Africa	ZAF	44	42	67	72	69	5
Brazil	BRA	43	42	69	72	69	3
Bulgaria	BGR	43	41	69	77	75	8
Greece	GRC	43	40	69	80	94	11
Italy	ITA	43	43	69	69	72	0
Romania	ROM	43	43	69	69	66	0
Senegal	SEN	43	41	69	77	94	8
Swaziland	SWZ	43	39	69	82	88	13
Montenegro	MON	42	44	76	67	75	-9
Sao Tome and Principe	STP	42	42	76	72	72	-4
Serbia	SCG	41	42	78	72	80	-6
Tunisia	TUN	40	41	79	77	75	-2
Benin	BEN	39	36	80	94	94	14
Bosnia and Herzegovina	BIH	39	42	80	72	72	-8
El Salvador	SLV	39	38	80	83	83	3
Mongolia	MNG	39	38	80	83	94	3
Morocco	MAR	39	37	80	91	88	11
Burkina Faso	BFA	38	38	85	83	83	-2
India	IND	38	36	85	94	94	9
Jamaica	JAM	38	38	85	83	83	-2
Peru	PER	38	38	85	83	83	-2
Philippines	PHL	38	36	85	94	105	9
Sri Lanka	LKA	38	37	85	91	79	6
Thailand	THA	38	35	85	102	88	17
Trinidad and Tobago	TTO	38	38	85	83	80	-2
Zambia	ZMB	38	38	85	83	88	-2
Armenia	ARM	37	36	94	94	105	0
Colombia	COL	37	36	94	94	94	0
Egypt	EGY	37	32	94	114	118	20

Gabon	GAB	37	34	94	106	102	12
Liberia	LBR	37	38	94	83	75	-11
Panama	PAN	37	35	94	102	83	8
Algeria	DZA	36	36	100	94	105	-6
China	CHN	36	40	100	80	80	-20
Suriname	SUR	36	36	100	94	88	-6
Bolivia	BOL	35	34	103	106	105	3
Mexico	MEX	35	34	103	106	105	3
Moldova	MDA	35	35	103	102	94	-1
Niger	NER	35	34	103	106	113	3
Argentina	ARG	34	34	107	106	102	-1
Djibouti	DJI	34	36	107	94	94	-13
Indonesia	IDN	34	32	107	114	118	7
Albania	ALB	33	31	110	116	113	6
Ecuador	ECU	33	35	110	102	118	-8
Ethiopia	ETH	33	33	110	111	113	1
Kosovo	LWI	33	33	110	111	105	1
Malawi	MWI	33	37	110	91	88	-19
Côte d'Ivoire	CIV	32	27	115	136	130	21
Dominican Republic	DOM	32	29	115	123	118	8
Guatemala	GTM	32	29	115	123	113	8
Mali	MLI	32	28	115	127	105	12
Belarus	BLR	31	29	119	123	123	4
Mozambique	MOZ	31	30	119	119	123	0
Sierra Leone	SLE	31	30	119	119	123	0
Tanzania	TZA	31	33	119	111	102	-8
Vietnam	VNM	31	31	119	116	123	-3
Guyana	GUY	30	27	124	136	133	12
Mauritania	MRT	30	30	124	119	123	-5
Azerbaijan	AZE	29	28	126	127	139	1
Gambia	GMB	29	28	126	127	105	1

Honduras	HND	29	26	126	140	133	14
Kazakhstan	KAZ	29	26	126	140	133	14
Nepal	NPL	29	31	126	116	139	-10
Pakistan	PAK	29	28	126	127	139	1
Togo	TGO	29	29	126	123	128	-3
Madagascar	MDG	28	28	133	127	118	-6
Nicaragua	NIC	28	28	133	127	130	-6
Timor-Leste	TLS	28	30	133	119	113	-14
Cameroon	CMR	27	25	136	144	144	8
Iran	IRN	27	25	136	144	133	8
Kyrgyzstan	KGZ	27	24	136	150	154	14
Lebanon	LBN	27	28	136	127	128	-9
Nigeria	NGA	27	25	136	144	139	8
Russia	RUS	27	28	136	127	133	-9
Comoros	COM	26	28	142	127	133	-15
Uganda	UGA	26	26	142	140	130	-2
Ukraine	UKR	26	25	142	144	144	2
Bangladesh	BGD	25	27	145	136	144	-9
Guinea	GIN	25	24	145	150	154	5
Kenya	KEN	25	27	145	136	139	-9
Laos	LAO	25	26	145	140	160	-5
Papua New Guinea	PNG	25	25	145	144	150	-1
Central African Republic	CAF	24	25	150	144	144	-6
Paraguay	PRY	24	24	150	150	150	0
Congo Republic	COG	23	22	152	154	144	2
Tajikistan	TJK	23	22	152	154	157	2
Chad	TCD	22	19	154	163	165	9
Democratic Republic of the Congo	COD	22	22	154	154	160	0
Cambodia	KHM	21	20	156	160	157	4

Myanmar	MMR	21	21	156	157	172	1
Zimbabwe	ZWE	21	21	156	157	163	1
Burundi	BDI	20	21	159	157	165	-2
Syria	SYR	20	17	159	168	144	9
Angola	AGO	19	23	161	153	157	-8
Guinea-Bissau	GNB	19	19	161	163	150	2
Haiti	HTI	19	19	161	163	165	2
Venezuela	VEN	19	20	161	160	165	-1
Yemen	YEM	19	18	161	167	156	6
Eritrea	ERI	18	20	166	160	150	-6
Libya	LBY	18	15	166	172	160	6
Uzbekistan	UZB	18	17	166	168	170	2
Turkmenistan	TKM	17	17	169	168	170	-1
Iraq	IRQ	16	16	170	171	169	1
South Sudan	SSD	15	14	171	173	#N/A	2
Afghanistan	AFG	12	8	172	175	174	3
Sudan	SDN	11	11	173	174	173	1
Korea (North)	PRK	8	8	174	175	174	1
Somalia	SOM	8	8	174	175	174	1

While going through the above data, it is apparent that corruption is a major problem in the world, both developed and developing countries. Denmark, New Zealand and Finland are the countries which may be called as the lesser corruption zone. Why there is slighter corruption than other countries, we have to recognize the culture of those countries. At this juncture we shall discuss only Denmark country:

DENMARK CULTURE AND HISTORY

Denmark was occupied by Germany till 9th April, 1940. It was freed on 5th May, 1945. When the liberation was announced in the 8.30

pm BBC broadcast on 4th May, 1945, many Danes spontaneously placed lit candles on their window sills. This became a custom that is still kept up by many Danes. Denmark population is 5.6 crore only. According to Tom Norris, Ambassador of Denmark, corruption is broadly defined as abusively exploiting entrusted power/funds for personal gain. It's bribery, illegal payments and facilitation payments, the last one sometimes legal, sometimes not!

Corruption violates everyone whose life, daily activities and happiness depend on the integrity of the authorities and public officials. It threatens stability and safety and undermines democratic institutions and values, and still corruption is widespread across the world.

As you may know Transparency International concluded in its 2012 study that Denmark, along with New Zealand and Finland, is the least corrupt country in the world. In fact Denmark has always ranked as a country of low corruption. As an official representative of my country, I am, of course, proud of that.

The following reasons were given for least corruption in that country:

- Danes are not willing to pay bribe or to accept it
- Danes are better people and their morality is very high
- They are lucky that their ancestors are anti-corrupt and it is in their genes
- They are more ethical and not immune to corruption
- High degree of trust on one another
- Integrity in payment of high tax for welfare of the state
- Danes do not have to pay for their children to go to primary school or high school and they do not save for

years to put their children through university. They do not need insurance to go to hospital, get medication or see a doctor, and if they lose their job, relatively generous unemployment benefits are supplied by a combination of insurance and public funds. The elderly do not need insurance and do not have to pay out of their pocket to get the necessary help with cleaning or personal assistance, and most of the costs associated with day care for children are also tax-financed. In other words, one does not have to put money aside for bad times as you will be provided for.

- Fair working conditions, social security, health arrangements, decent salaries and pension schemes are among the things that contribute to giving the Danes reasonable living conditions
- In Denmark they have a very inclusive political culture as well, and both public and private institutions are highly transparent, which makes it easier to hold, for instance, politicians or companies responsible for irregularities
- Media has a very defining roll
- Both the Danish Government and the Danish Federation of Industries, the Danish companies' own branch organization, have signaled quite clearly that corruption under all circumstances is unacceptable – the Danish Federation of Industries has, indeed, made it clear that they have a "zero tolerance".

The above speech of Mr. Norris speaks the story of Denmark and it is obvious that there is zero tolerance power against corruption. Ethic and moral values of each person and even media has a well-defined role. When all such things are prevailing in any country, corruption cannot arise.

STORY OF FINLAND IN FIGHT AGAINST CORRUPTION

The war on corruption is now a required course in the "school of good governance" the world over. In Central America hardly anybody has enrolled so far, but perhaps we can learn some generic lessons from Finland's positive experience, even given the differences in its political class, government officials, ***population, culture and history.*** The main strength was — and still is — the establishment and maintenance of a social order that offers no fertile ground for corruption to take root.

Finland's social order is characterized by specific strengths, particularly moderation, self-control and a sense of common good. The result is a society that morally and legally condemns the centralization of power and socio-economic disparities, promoting a culture of governance that fosters the common good. Research has shown a correlation between a high degree of trust among the members of a society and low levels of corruption. Their private sector has also maintained the value of responsibility, honesty and fair play. Ethical education has become an integral component of the Finnish Business Administration training. A full 90% of Finnish business executives consider that obeying the law is essential in their corporate activities. In nutshell, we conclude that:

- Their ethics and morality are very high
- Concern and maintenance of social discipline
- They believe in no centralization of power
- High degree of trust among one another

It can be concluded that where ethics, morality, discipline, trust and integrity are high, the level of corruption automatically drops.

History of corruption in India is very old but here we shall be limited to recent phase.

During World War II, Mahatma Gandhi and Jawaharlal Nehru took a serious concern of the growing corruption in the Congress. Mahatma Gandhi clearly said, "I would go to the length of giving the whole Congress organization a decent burial, rather than put up corruption that is rampant." Its level was rising during the year 1939-45.

When India was freed from the British in the year 1947, they chose planning model to develop the country. During the planning process, some of the important decisions taken by India are as under:

- Setting up of public sector
- Nationalization of banks and insurance
- Public Distribution System
- Permit and licence raj
- Panchayati Raj
- Rationing
- Establishment of various departments
- Social welfare scheme, MGNREGA, etc.

Thus, all the command is with the Government departments, which provide opportunity to exhort money from aggrieved persons. Here the corruption level starts from higher to bottom and bottom to the higher levels. In some of the departments like PWD and Tehsils, etc. corruption is in a much-planned way. It is like a cancer which is very difficult to cure.

The modus operandi and type of corruption adopted by various persons in this field are also unusual which can be enumerated as under:

MUTUAL OR CONSENTED CORRUPTION

This may be called as willing and planner corruption. Both of the parties agree for unlawful activity. One party agrees for prompt clearance of the file and the other is willing to offer money for seeking such a favour. When the agreement is complete; this may be called as mutual corruption. This type of corruption is very dangerous in a society and shows poor ethical and moral values of our society.

POLITICAL CORRUPTION

As per the Transparency International Organization, "Political corruption is the abuse of entrusted power by political leaders for private gain. The scale of the problem can be vast. One of the world's most corrupt leaders, Mohamed Suharto of Indonesia, allegedly embezzled up to US $35 billions in a country with a GDP of less than US $700 per capita.

Corruption in political finance takes many forms, ranging from vote buying and the use of illicit funds to the sale of appointments and the abuse of state resources. Not all are illegal. Legal donations to political parties often result in policy changes. A 2003 World Economic Forum survey finds that in 89 per cent of the 102 countries surveyed the direct influence of legal political donations on specific policy outcomes is moderate or high.

Indian political scene has the same impact. This is the most important organ which has promoted corruption in politics. Examples are: various scams by political leaders, links with industrial and business classes, undue interference in the administration, huge election expenses, recruitment scandals, kidnapping and to win in elections, use of liquor, wealth and everything among the people, horse-trading of MPs and MLAs at the time of formation of a government. This impact has an adverse effect on the administrative machinery.

FORCED CORRUPTION

Forced corruption is where takers forcefully demand money and the giver offers the money in compulsion. There are a number of cases. Out of this corruption some of the cases go to the Police Department, the CBI or any other grievances department.

PRESSURE CORRUPTION FROM CLIENTS

It has been observed that some of the work cannot be done by the authority due to some rules and regulations. In such cases clients pressurize the organization/officer concerned by complaining that so and so officer is demanding money.

SOCIAL AND ECONOMIC CORRUPTION

It includes corruption in social schemes such as Welfare of Scheduled Caste and Tribe schemes, EWS scheme, Health schemes, bank loans, old-age pension schemes, etc.

MEDICAL CORRUPTION

Sale of human organs, illegal abortion, illegal sex identification, passing of wrong samples of medicines, practice in private hospitals, loot in operation charges, selling of duplicate medicines are the examples of such corruption.

SECULAR AND SPIRITUAL CORRUPTION

There are various types of committees in the religious institutions and no accounts are being maintained by them. Even spiritual healers have not escaped from this type of corruption. Donations in the name of religion are very common. No free social welfare activity is done by most of the secular and spiritual leaders.

Other types of corruption may be described as participation in games corruption, bureaucrat's corruption, media and entertainment industry corruption.

DETAIL OF PENDING CORRUPTION CASES

On 31st January, 2013, the Minister of State for Personnel, Public Grievances and Pensions, Shri V. Narayanasamy, said in response to a written question that over 6,800 corruption cases are pending in various special CBI courts across the country with the highest number of such pending cases in the National Capital.

DATA OF CORRUPTION CASES

The Press information Bureau, Government of India, Ministry of Personnel, Public Grievances and Pension, provided the information received from the Central Vigilance Commission (CVC), details of cases received and disposed during the last five years in respect of Central Government employees (including employees of the Central public sector enterprises (CPSEs), public sector banks (PSBs), financial institutions (FIs), autonomous bodies, etc. under the Central Government.

Data of Corruption Cases

S. No.	Year	No. of cases received	No. of cases disposed
1	2010	5327	5522
2	2011	5573	5341
3	2012	5528	5720
4	2013	5423	4801
5	2014	5492**	5867**

** ***Figures for 2014 are tentative. The data are based on the annual reports submitted by the CVOs. For the year 2013, 264 organizations and for the year 2014, 206 organizations have submitted annual reports and the above information relates to only those organizations.***

As per information received from the CBI, a total of 3,296 cases have been registered under the Prevention of Corruption Act, 1988, during the last six years i.e. 2010, 2011, 2012, 2013, 2014 and 2015 (up to 31.03.2015). The year-wise break-up of number of cases registered during the above said period with present status of these cases are attached as follows:-

Year	No. of PC Act cases registered	No. of cases charge-sheeted	No. of persons convicted
2010	580	541	80
2011	600	456	45
2012	703	509	35
2013	649	439	8
2014	611	235	1
2015	153	7	0
Total	3296	2187	169

The above CBI report provides information about the magnitude and intensity of corruption in India. The volume of complaints received and cases registered during the year is too much. The number of cases registered by the CBI from 2010 to 2015 is 3,296, of which 2,187 persons are charge-sheeted and 169 convicted.

REASONS OF CORRUPTION PROTECTION TO GOVERNMENT EMPLOYEES

Nowadays, it is the main concern of most of the youth and individuals to acquire Government-related jobs. The reasons behind are less work, absolute powers and security of job. The CVC and the CBI are the watchdog of these departments to control corruption but the departmental proceedings are so lengthy and difficult that it is very difficult to take strict action against the erring officials. Though a citizen chart and time limit are prescribed for each work, nobody is taking note of this, which may cause corruption.

LACK OF STRONG WILL AGAINST CORRUPTION

We, the people of India, ourselves are not willing to eradicate corruption on war footings. In view of our own interest, people fulfill the demands of takers. Thus, there is lack of determination to remove corruption in our country.

CORRUPTION THROUGH INTERMEDIARIES

Departments like the Railways, the Public Works Department, Tehsils, Health, etc. entertain the intermediaries which give an opportunity to extort money from the public.

LACK OF HONEST AND POSITIVE LEADERSHIP

Honest with positive leadership is required. In the absence of this, the corruption level may rise.

ADMINISTRATIVE MACHINERY

In the absence of responsibility, accountability and poor monitoring of the decision-making process, corruption may escalate.

EXCESSIVE RULES AND REGULATIONS

The procedure of the Government even in respect of simple things like ration card, permit, old-age pension, driving licence and vehicle registration certificates are not so easy, which provide ample opportunity to extort money from public. Lack of transparency and complicated procedures further increase corruption.

OTHER REASONS

This may be described as lack of transparency, habit of delaying work and lack of knowledge in the field.

HOW TO CONTROL CORRUPTION

The question arises whether corruption from the world will be eradicated or not. Probably, not so easily. Transparency International has suggested the following methods, especially for India:

- Appointment of Lok Ayuktas (state-level Ombudsmen) in all States.

- Compulsory audit of accounts of political parties.
- Electoral reforms to prevent tainted politicians from contesting elections and holding the position of power.
- Enactment of legislation for forfeiture of illegally acquired property.
- Speedy trial of criminal cases against ministers, MPs and MLAs.

It is a matter of some relief that there was improvement in the ranking. As per Transparency International India (TII) data, India has showed some improvement in addressing corruption this year, ranking 85 among 175 countries as against 94 last year. The report noted that with the new Government in office, the CPI possibly captured the anti-corruption mandate on which the new Government was elected and the possibility of some new reforms in this area. "However, the data used for the CPI mostly was collected prior to the change of Government and, therefore, this will not reflect directly into any of the CPI sources." Anti-corruption campaign in India led by veteran activist Anna Hazare and the People of India is also the result of improvement in the ranking.

Shri N. Vittal (2001) concluded that "corruption cannot be eradicated without curbing political corruption as it starts from top and trickles down to the bottom".

Corruption can be restricted by the following methods:

- Online payment to all persons, including salary, contractor or any type of payment or donations. The Central Government is also using this technique in most of the departments. The States should also use this method to combat corruption. Thus, information technology can play a vital role to restrict corruption. To some extent, the Government of India got success.

- Simplification of rules and regulations will also be helpful to combat corruption
- Feedback system from the clients/persons
- Have a strong will of people against corruption
- Stop mutual corruption with wide publicity
- The most important is the maintenance of social regulation, ethics and morality
- Decentralization of power
- Reward for honesty
- Punishment for false complainants
- Timely punishment to corrupt officials
- Special vigil of the Revenue Department, Health Department, Police Department, PWD, Income Tax and Excise Departments and Judiciary.
- No doubt, democracy is good for the country, but it should be with discipline.
- Maintenance of efficiency and proper citizen chart in Judiciary.
- Restrict commercialization of education.
- To some extent, media and political opponents are exposing India for their self interest.
- Audit objections must be foolproof after verification of the contents and keeping in view the commercial interests also but not on assumption basis.
- Big push to the Lok Pal Bill
- Appointment of Lok Ayukatas at the earliest

IMPORTANT CASES OF CORRUPTION/SCAMS

It should not have come as a big surprise that the allegations of corruption began immediately after Independence against well-known political personalities and even Ministers.

COAL GATE SCAM-2012

As per the CAG report, firms are likely to gain Rs. 1.86 lakh crore from coal blocks that were allocated to them on nomination basis instead of competitive bidding, which amounted to loss to the national exchequer.

The CAG, in its report, tabled in Parliament, named 25 companies, including Essar Power, Hindalco, Tata Steel, Tata Power and Jindal Steel and Power, which have got the blocks in various states.

2-G SCAM

The illegal undercharging by Government officials of various telecom companies during the allocation of 2G licences for cell phone subscriptions gave rise to the 2G spectrum scam. According to the CAG, the scam amounts to about Rs 1,76,000 crore.

CWG SCAM

Commonwealth Games is perhaps one of India's most well-known scam. Suresh Kalmadi, who was the Chairman of the Organizing Committee of the Commonwealth Games, was the main accused. It consisted of a number of corrupt deals involving overstated contracts. Kalmadi also handed out a Rs 141-crore contract to

Swiss Timing for its timing equipment; the deal was inflated by Rs 95 crore. Less than 10 days before the games, athletes were asked to move into apartments that were shabby and dilapidated.

FODDER SCAM

This scam broke out in 1996 in the town of Chaibasa when the Animal Husbandry Department embezzled funds of around Rs 950 crore meant to purchase cattle fodder, medicines and animal husbandry equipment in Bihar. Lalu Prasad Yadav, the Chief Minister of the State, was forced to resign along with former Chief Minister, Jagannath Mishra.

TELGI AND STAMP PAPER SCAM

Abdul Karim Telgi's fake paper scam, which was discovered in 2003, estimated a loss of Rs. 30,000 crore for the country. The linchpin began to counterfeit stamp paper which led to the multi-crore scam. He sold fake stamp papers to individuals, banks, insurance companies and share-broking firms through 300 agents.

HARSHAD MEHTA SCAM

Harshad Mehta, popularly called the Big Bull among traders, who triggered a trend in the stock market before his scam worth Rs. 4,000 crore, was exposed in 1992. He used the funds from inter-bank transactions to buy shares at a premium across many sectors.

SATYAM SCAM

Satyam Computers chief B. Ramalinga Raju misappropriated books and inflated figures which led to a scam that incurred a loss of Rs 8,000 crore.

BOFORS SCAM

The Bofors scam, which is sometimes referred to as India's Watergate Scandal, gave rise to a hullabaloo in the country pointing fingers at Rajiv Gandhi, who was the Prime Minister then, for receiving a bribe from Bofors AB, a Swedish company. The estimation of the scam amounted to Rs. 64 crore. The Government of India and the Bofors signed a contract in 1986 for the supply of 155mm Howitzer field guns. About a year later the Swedish radio alleged that Bofors paid kickbacks to politicians and defence officials to close the deal. However, the Howitzer guns proved to be of high standard and played a very important role in the victory of the Kargil war.

HAWALA SCAM

The hawala scandal involved payments totaling Rs. 1,000 crore, which were allegedly received by politicians through four hawala brokers, the Jain brothers, and accusations were leveled against some of the country's leading politicians like L.K. Advani, V.C. Shukla, P. Shiv Shankar, Sharad Yadav, Balram Jakhar and Madan Lal Khurana. It was alleged that terrorist outfits in Kashmir received funds by this means.

OTHER SCAMS

1. Jeep Purchase (1948): Free India's corruption graph begins. V.K. Krishna Menon, then Indian High Commissioner to Britain, bypassed protocol to sign a deal worth Rs. 80 lakh with a foreign firm for the purchase of Army jeeps. The case was closed in 1955 and soon after Menon joined the Nehru Cabinet.

2. Cycle Imports (1951): S.A. Venkataraman, then Secretary, Ministry of Commerce and Industry, was jailed for accepting a bribe in lieu of granting a cycle import quota to a company.

3. BHU Funds (1956): In one of the first instances of corruption in educational institutions, Benaras Hindu University officials were accused of misappropriation of funds worth Rs 50 lakh.

4. Mundhra scandal (1957): It was the media that first hinted that there might be a scam involving the sale of shares to the LIC. Feroz Gandhi sources the confidential correspondence between then Finance Minister T.T. Krishnamachari and his Principal Finance Secretary, and raised a question in Parliament on the sale of "fraudulent" shares to the LIC by a Calcutta-based Marwari businessman named Haridas Mundhra. Prime Minister Jawaharlal Nehru set up a one-man commission headed by Justice M.C. Chagla to investigate the matter when it became evident that there was a prima facie case. Chagla concluded that Mundhra had sold fictitious shares to the LIC, thereby defrauding the insurance company to the tune of Rs. 1.25 crore. Mundhra was sentenced to 22

years in prison. The scam also forced the resignation of T.T. Krishnamachari.

5. Kairon Scam (1963): Partap Singh Kairon, who is called father of the modern Punjab, became the first Indian Chief Minister in 1956 to be accused of abusing power for his own benefit and that of his sons and relatives. The questionable estimated amount was around Rs. 1 crore, a very good amount those days. However, he had to quit a year later.

6. Antulay Trust (1981): With the exposure of this scandal concerning A.R. Antulay, then Chief Minister of Maharashtra, The Indian Express was reborn. Antulay had garnered Rs. 30 crore from businesses dependent on state resources like cement and kept the money in a private trust.

7. St Kitts Forgery (1989): An attempt was made to sully V.P. Singh's "Mr Clean" image by forging documents to allege that he was a beneficiary of his son Ajeya Singh's account in the First Trust Corp. at St Kitts with a deposit of $21 millions.

8. JMM Bribes (1995): Jharkhand Mukti Morcha leader Shailendra Mahato testified that he and three party members received bribes of Rs. 30 lakh to bail out the P.V. Narasimha Rao government in the 1993 No-Confidence Motion.

9. Telecom Scam (1996): Former Minister of State for Communication Sukh Ram was accused of causing a loss of Rs. 1.6 crore to the exchequer by favouring a Hyderabad-based private firm in the purchase of telecom equipment. He, along with two others, was convicted in 2002.

10. Fodder Scam (1996): The Accountant General's concerns about the withdrawal of excess funds by Bihar's Animal Husbandry Department unveiled a Rs. 950-crore scam involving Lalu Prasad Yadav, then Chief Minister. He resigned a year later.

11. CRB Scam (1997): Another scam forged by greed and discovered through accident. Chain Roop Bhansali, a smart-talking entrepreneur, created a pyramid financial empire based on high-cost financing. At its peak, his Rs. 1,000-crore financial conglomerate had in its ranks a mutual fund, a financial services company into fixed deposits, and a merchant bank. Bhansali knew how to work the system became evident when he also managed to secure a provisional banking licence. Then his luck ran out. An executive in the State Bank of India inadvertently discovered that some interest warrants issued by Bhansali were not backed by cash. The bubble finally burst in May 1997, but by that time investors had lost over Rs. 1,000 crore. This was among the first retail scams in India and it was played out, in smaller avatars, across the country, especially in the South where financial services companies promised returns in excess of 20 per cent and decamped with the principal. Bhansali was arrested for a few weeks and later released on bail.

FUTURE OF CORRUPTION IN INDIA

As per TII data, India has improved its ranking to 85 from 94 in the year 2014. This may be due to the result of the "India Against Corruption Movement" by Shri Anna Hazare, Arvind Kejriwal, Sri Sri Ravi Shankar, Mrs Kiran Bedi and youth of India.

The time has come when everybody is prepared to fight the sin of corruption and it is the need of the hour "to eradicate corruption from the blood of individuals". The Government of India has started to work in this direction. If its intention is still skeptical, people of India have the capacity to get the work done from them. I am sure that it will certainly take years, if not decades, to eradicate corruption. In the past the reason of corruption was low down salary of Government employees. Now due to revision in pay scales, employees get handsome salaries as per Indian standards. Politicians are also getting good amount of salary and pension. Big guns among the leaders have gone to prison or will go to prison.

The Government is doing its best to fill the vacancies of judge to enable them to dispose all related cases at the earliest. The Government is doing all efforts in the entire field. E-governance, Digital India, I.T. Department, NEFT, RTGS, Debit Card, Credit Card system and Financial Inclusion of all people will certainly improve the ranking of India in near future. Thus, ready for subdued corruption by 2030.

Thus, we are confident that in the coming few years, E-governance, I.T. techniques, ethical and moral values of people, efforts of Transparency International, the Right to Information Act, Digital India, Social Media and effective judiciary will be so powerful that nobody will have the courage to give and take money so easily and eradication of this evil looks certain.

CHAPTER 7

COMMUNAL DISHARMONY AND INTOLERANCE

A nation, which goes 100 steps forward to develop the country, can go 70 steps backward in case there are frequent incidents of communal violence and intolerance among the people of that nation.

Communal harmony, religion and discrimination on the basis of caste and creed are inter-related. A slight imbalance between them can spoil any nation.

The country like the United Kingdom, the USA, Russia, France and Germany also not untouched from the evil of communal disharmony and intolerance. Discrimination is common in these countries.

India, Pakistan, Bangladesh and Sri Lanka have state effects of this imbalance.

India is a Secular State and the people of different religions are living in a friendly atmosphere. But sometimes it has been observed that small issues take the shape of riots and communal violence. Nowadays, these types of incidents are increasing day by day not only in India but in the whole world.

To study this aspect, we should scrutinize the population base of every religion as on 2011 being a secular country.

Table I

Religion	Number (crore) 2001-11	%age
All religion	121.08	
Hindus	96.63	79.80
Muslims	17.22	13.2
Christians	2.78	2.3
Sikhs	2.08	1.7
Buddhists	0.84	0.7
Jains	0.45	0.4
Others	1.08	0.89

Source: Census data

DECADAL POPULATION GROWTH

Table II

Religion	1991	2001	2011
Hindus	25.1	20.3	16.8
Muslims	34.5	29.5	24.6
Christians	21.5	22.6	15.5
Sikhs	24.3	18.2	8.4
Buddhists	35.3	24.5	6.1
Jains	4.6	26	5.4

The above data speak that India now has 96.63 crore Hindus, who make up 79.8 per cent of its population, and 17.22 crore Muslims, who make up 13.20 per cent. Among the other minorities, Christians make up 2.3 per cent of the population and Sikhs 1.71 per cent.

The distribution of data is of the total population by six major religious communities — Hindu, Muslim, Christian, Sikh,

Buddhist and Jain, besides "other religions and persuasions" and "religion not stated".

If we look at the growth rate we shall come across that the Hindu population is growing at 16.80%, whereas the Muslim population is growing at 24.60% rate. The trend is clear that the Muslim population is growing slower than it had in the previous decades, and its growth rate has slowed more sharply than that of the Hindus, new Census data show. As the literacy rate is increasing among the Muslims, the population is decreasing.

Being a Secular State, it is the responsibility of the majority Government and population to safeguard the interest of the minority communities.

Since India is a democratic country and there is extreme freedom of speech, which makes politicians, majority and minority communities and even terrorists and criminals take the benefit of disorderliness of democracy which causes riots and strikes and communal disturbance in the country. Whenever any election is declared or any issue arises, all the politicians do not hesitate to use every modus operandi to please the minority or majority community.

In brief, the reason of communal violence may be described as confrontation with two or more communities which may later take the shape of communal riots.

Other reasons are cow protection, disrespect to religious books, provocation by terrorist organizations, enemy countries, change of religion or similar type of causes.

Thus, we can conclude that these clashes arise from minor events and take the major shape due to intolerance. It is a matter of shame that if we see the number of communal riots, they are countless. We give hereunder some of the major riots which occurred in India after Independence:

MAJOR RIOTS SINCE 1947

Desri Ground massacre (part of the terrorist incident	28 March 1986	Ludhiana	13
Mallian massacre (part of the) Terrorist incident	29 March 1986	Jalandhar	20
Bus Passenger massacre IV-Terrorist incident)	30 November 1986	Khudda, Punjab	24
Hashimpura massacre	22 May 1987	Meerut. {imkan	42
Bus Passenger massacre V (part of the terrprost incident	July 1987	Fatehabad, Haryana	80
Bhagalpur Incident	October 1989	Bihar	The total dead numbered around 1000,.
Ethnic cleansing of Hindu Pandits	1990s	Jammu and Kashmir	219-399
Gawakadal-massacre	20 January 1990	Srinagar	50
Train Passengers)	15 June 1988	Ludhiana	80
Train Passenger massacre III	December 1988	Ludhiana	49
Bombay Riots	December 1992 - January 1993	Mumbai	900

SOPORE INCIDENTS	6 January 1993	Kashmir	55
Bijbehara Massacre	October 22, 1993	Kashmir	55
Laxaman Masscare	1 December 1997	Bihar	58
Amarnath Pilgimerge Massacre	1 August 2000	J&K	30
Kishtwar Massacre	3 August 2001	J&K	19
Godhara Massacre	27 February 2002	Godhra, Gujarat	59
Gujarat violence	28 February 2002	Ahmedabad	2,044
Gulbarg Society Incident	28 February 2002	Ahmedabad	69
Naroda violence	28 February 2002	Ahmedabad	97
Raghunath Hindu temple massacre I)	30 March 2002	J&K	11
Akshardham incident	24 September 2002	Gujarat	29
Varanasi Bombing	March 2006	U P	28
Doda Massacre	30 April 2006	J&K	35
Samjhauta Express Massacre	18 February 2007	Diwana station	68
Kandhamal riots	August 2008	Orrisa	42
Mumbai Massacre	26 November 2008	Mumbai	164+(11 Attacker) & (600+ Injuries)
Dantewada Bombing	17 May 2010	Chattishgarh	76
Assam Violence	July 2012	Assam	77 deaths
Muzaffarnagar Incidents	25 August 2013 - 17 September 2013	U.P	62

Though the above data are not foolproof and no exact record and reasons of conflicts are available, it is clear that these conflicts are common in India, resulting in a huge burden on the exchequer of the Government. Today, if we are eager to enter the 21st century with clean hand, we, the people of India, have to make a tolerance and improvement in ourselves.

To control such type of violence, the Government of India has already passed the Bills in 2005. The highlights of the above Bills are as under:

- The Communal Violence (Prevention, Control and Rehabilitation of Victims) Bill, 2005, provides for (a) prevention and control of communal violence, (b) speedy investigation and trials, and (c) rehabilitation of victims.
- The State Governments can declare an area as communally disturbed under certain conditions. The District Magistrate or the competent authority appointed by a State Government can take measures such as regulating assembly, directing persons to deposit their arms, searching premises, etc. to control communal violence.
- The Bill provides for double the punishment as provided by other existing laws. The State Governments shall establish special courts to try offences under this law. These courts may direct convicted persons to pay compensation to victims or dependents.
- Communal Disturbance Relief and Rehabilitation Councils will be formed at the national, state and district levels.
- The District Council shall pay at least 20 per cent of total compensation as immediate step

The other key features of the Bills are:

- Prevention and control of communal violence
- Investigation and punishment of offences under the Act.
- Relief and rehabilitation
- Declaration of an area as communally disturbed.
- Accountability of public servant
- Witness protection

To some extent, the above rules can forcibly control the communal disturbances, but ethically the following rules must be adopted to control the clashes:

- Political tolerance by political leaders
- Religious tolerance by all religious persons
- To increase the literacy among the communities
- Moderate approach towards religions
- Democratic discipline
- Positive media approach
- Heavy Punishment to guilty
- PUBLIC PROPERTY SHOULD NOT BE ALLOWED TO DESTROYED BY RIOTERS.

In view of the increasing communal tolerance, Lok Sabha of India took up a debate on December 1, 2015. All the leaders including Rahul Gandhi presented their view points on the recent intolerance of writers, Dadri incidents, Dalits etc, but the outcome of the meeting was only discussion.

On the same day while addressing the graduaates students of Gujarat Vidyapeeth, an institution founded by Mahatama

Gandhi, in 1920, Hon'ble Pranav Mukharjee, President of India said,"Gandhiji in life and in death struggled for communal harmony. Education in peace and harmony is the key to contain and reorient the disruptive forces in society,".

He also hinted at the uproar over the perceived intolerance in the country. He asked people to keep their minds clean of dirt.

"The real dirt of India lies not in our streets but in our minds and in our unwillingness to let go of views that divide society into 'them' and 'us', 'pure' and 'impure'. We must make a success of the Swachh Bharat Mission," said Mukherj.

In the concluding remarks, Home Minister of India said, "that in Islamic countries, different sects of islam fought against each other whereas in India people belonging to different religion lived in peace and harmony barring a few stray incidents". He further remarked that anybody trying to disturb the harmony would not be spared.

From the above discussion, one thing is rather clear that India is a demoractic country and there is no question of intolerance in our countries. Whenever any problem arise, such things may overcome through healthy discussions.

If we see all around the world, No COUNTRY is escaped from communal disharmony. It is pertinent to mention here that India is a country of different religions, different culture and different linguel society. It is known as Tolerant country. Now a days, frequent discussion on intolerance is on the line, which is completely vague and in any way cannot come under the purview of our nation. Communal and Secular incidents comes and goes but India is going on with overcomes of all hurdles.

India is on the right path of Mahatama Gandhi. Next century is India's century. In view of deep rooted democracy and nature of our constitution, it will be very difficult for communal forces to regain their power and and It is sure there will be no communal intolerance by 2030.

....

ABOUT THE AUTHOR

Rajendra Sharma was born and brought up in India in Haryana in 1955. Mr. Sharma graduated and postgraduated from Punjab University, Chandigarh. He is also fellow from Insurance Institute of India and retired as Class-I executive from an insurance company. He married in the year 1981 and has two children who have interest in computer research and IT field. Members of family inspired him and helped him for concentration which is resulted in the shape of book. This book will be helpful for coming generation.

From the start of life, Mr. Sharma has had an interest in analytical study of any subject. After being inspired by this, Mr. Sharma chose to analyse the problem of countries and their solutions. The problems mentioned in the book are like a mirror of India, and he is sure that India will prevail upon all the problems by 2047.

This book will prove to be a boon for the future generations.

REFERENCES

CHAPTER 1

1. Extract of Nehru's speech
2. India Since Independence - Publication Division Ministry of Information & Broadcasting - edition revised by S.P. Agarwal.
3. Budget speech of Shri R.K. Shanmukhan Chetty, Ministry of Finance introducing the Budget 1947-48.
4. Extract of Chapter 38 of the Planning Commission - Ist Five-Year Plan.
5. mha/.nic.in/par 2013/par 2014-pdfs/ls-280715/1256/pdf
6. Tyranny of Partition - Kathinka Sinha - Extract P-142- 143

CHAPTER 2

1. India.govt.in/mygovernment/constitution india.
2. Extract from An Introduction to India's Constitution and Constitutional Law - Subhash C. Kashyap.-2001
3. Clear IAS.com/mustknowarticles-of-India-constitution.

CHAPTER 3

1. eands.dacnet.nic/in/publication-Directorate of Economics and Statistics site.D-I-101
2. MORTH_roadtransport year book 2011-12.pdf.
3. Extract from India since independence

4. Hellotravel.com/stories-Mega dams of India (only data)
5. http://www.idea.int/vt/countryview.cfm?id=105(No.of voters)
6. Extract from India tomorrow-Dr Parmod Sharma.
7. Tribune newspaper dated 21/11/2015 https://swachhbharaturban.gov.in
8. /http://pmindia.gov.in/en/news updates/pm-launches-make-in-india-global-initiative/

CHAPTER 4

1. Extract-key finding-world population prospectus
2. Cenus India.govt.in
3. Population commission.nic.in

CHAPTER 5

1. http/Indiabudget.nic.in
2. Extract from the report of expert group to review methodology of poverty – Government of India - Planning Commission 2014 - C. Rangarajan Report.
3. Planning Commission.nic.in-9th Five-Year Plan - Volume 2
4. Www.nrega.nic.in
5. Planning Commission.nic.in/plans/mta/11th/chp 12 rural programme
6. www.who.int/trade/glossary/story028/en.
7. www.sksindia.com/Report Committee-Financial Inclusionn2008.

CHAPTER 6

1. http://www.theindependentindia.com/p/list-of-scams-in-india.html(OTHER SCAMS) extracts
2. https://in.finance.yahoo.com/photos/revealed-india-s-major-SCAMS
3. http://indiatoday.intoday.in/story/pm-cag-reports-manmohan-singh-oppostion/1/213492.html(COAL GATE)
4. http://pib.nic.in/newsite/PrintRelease.aspx?relid=120035(Corruption data) CBI AND VIG. DATA.
5. Ref: ttps://www.transparency.org/research/gcr/gcr_political_corruption/0/

CHAPTER 7

1. ww.prsindia.org/uploads/media/1167470057/legis1167477972_legislative_brief_communal_violence_bill_2005_FINAL.pdf
2. https://en.wikipedia.org/wiki/Religious_violence_in_India
3. censusindia.gov.in/Census_And_You/religion.aspx

Printed in the United States
By Bookmasters